ST. CUTHBERT AND DURHAM CATHEDRAL A CELEBRATION

Edited by
Douglas Pocock

Contributors:

Rosalind Billingham
Sherban Cantacuzino
Ian Curry
Roger Norris

David Park
Alan Piper
Douglas Pocock
Malcolm Thurlby

Foreword by

The Very Rev. John Arnold
Dean of Durham

Durham: City of Durham Trust

First published 1993 as *Durham Cathedral: A Celebration*
Second revised edition published 1995 by City of Durham Trust

Printed by Macdonald Press, Ltd., Spennymoor

ISBN 0 902776 04 5

Contents

Illustrations

Colour Plates

Cover: Durham Cathedral from South Street.
   I. Nave south aisle: dado arcade and 13th-century decorative painting, including chevrons on the respond.
  II. Refectory, east wall: detail of 12th-century paintings, showing a king and other figures. (Crown Copyright).
 III. Galilee Chapel, northern altar recess: St. Cuthbert, c.1180. (Crown Copyright).
  IV. Prior's Chapel (now Deanery): Adoration of the Child, c.1475-80. (Crown Copyright).
   V. Durham Cathedral, nave interior looking north-east.
  VI. Durham Cathedral looking east along the south aisle, watercolour by J.M.W. Turner, 1797-8.

VII. Durham Cathedral, watercolour by J.S. Cotman, 1806.

VIII. Durham, watercolour by Felix Mendelssohn Bartholdy, 1829.

IX. Cathedral, oil on canvas, by Maureen Enright, 1982.

X. God's Factory at night, gouache by Robert Soden, 1982.

Black and White

1. (a) Cathedral groundplan (b) Evolution of groundplan.
2. (a) Wanderings of St. Cuthbert Community.(b).Lands, estates, houses sometime attached to the Community
3. View from Observatory Field
4. View from Railway Station
5. View from below Prebends' Bridge.
6. View from below Framwellgate Bridge.
7. Longitudinal section of north side. (Plate I, Billings).
8. Longitudinal section of north side. (Plate II, Billings).
9. Section of transept to tower and east. (Billings).
10. Nine Altars: section to east., and plan. (Billings).
11. Winchester Cathedral, north transept looking NW.
12. Presbytery, looking SE.
13. Vault of north presbytery aisle, looking west.
14. Vault of fifth bay from crossing in nave south aisle.
15. Remains of wooden centring boards, nave south gallery.
16. Fragment of Romanesque vault web between Frosterly marble shaft and Gothic vault web, south presbytery.
17. South presbytery gallery, looking east.
18. North transept, looking NW.
19. North transept from south nave gallery.
20. North transept, looking SE.
21. North transept/north respond of east crossing arch from south presbytery gallery.
22. Coursing of SE high-vault capital, with east respond of north crossing arch, north transept.
23. Springer of high vault over bays 1 and 2 in east gallery, north transept.
24. Bays 1 and 2 of east side of south transept.
25. Bays 3 and 4 of east side of south transept.
26. Nave, north aisle, looking east.
27. Quadrant arches, before addition of two inner orders, nave south gallery (1843).
28. Nave vault, looking east.
29. Galilee chapel.
30. Nine Altars chapel, looking to north transept.
31. Lindisfarne Priory, nave south arcade.

32. Selby Abbey, nave south arcade.

33. Dunfermline Abbey, nave.

34. Kirkwall Cathedral, north presbytery aisle.

35. North front before 1660, with lead-covered spires on west towers.

36. North front, 1754, with "minerets" pencilled in by Thomas Wright, 1770.

37. North front, as proposed, 1777, drawn by George Nicholson.

38. East front of Chapel of Nine Altars, 1777, drawn by George Nicholson.

39. East front of Chapel of Nine Altars as proposed by James Wyatt, 1795.

40. Choir stalls and organ screen, 1680s to 1847.

41. Choir 1847-70, minus organ screen and with 17th century organ cut down and placed on north side.

42. Central tower proposals (a) James Wyatt, 1795, (b) Sir George Gilbert Scott, 1860.

43. Prior's Chapel (now Deanery): 13th-century foliate ornament on window jamb, based on Cufic lettering.

44. Galilee Chapel: damaged scene of the Coronation of the Virgin above the northern altar recess, with figure of St. Cuthbert blessing to the right (c.1300).

45. Galilee Chapel: Crucifixion (with Adam below rising from his grave and holding a chalice), flanked by the martyrdoms of SS. Peter and Paul(c.1300).

46. Galilee Chapel: Martyrdom of St. Paul (c.1300).

47. Tomb of Bishop Thomas Hatfield (d.1381): angel at the foot of the bishop's effigy.

48. Prior's Chapel (now Deanery): detail of the Resurrection (c.1475-80).

49. Durham Cathedral, watercolour by Thomas Hearne, 1783.

50. Durham Cathedral, watercolour by Edward Edwards, 1788.

51. Durham Cathedral and Bridge, watercolour by Thomas Girtin, 1799.

52. Durham Cathedral from the Bridge, watercolour by J.M.W. Turner, c.1798.

53. Durham Castle and Cathedral, watercolour by Thomas Girtin, 1799.

54. Durham Castle and Cathedral, watercolour by John Sell Cotman, c.1809-10.

55. Drawing from Tweed and Lakes Sketchbook, by J.M.W. Turner, 1797.

56. Drawing from Tweed and Lakes Sketchbook, by J.M.W. Turner, 1797.

57. Durham Cathedral, watercolour by J.M.W. Turner, c.1835.

58. Durham, watercolour by William Daniell, 1805.

59. Durham Cathedral from the River, watercolour by John Pearson, undated.

60. Durham Cathedral and Castle, watercolour by G.F. Robson, undated.

61. Durham Cathedral from Prebends' Bridge, watercolour by G.F. Robson, undated.

62. Durham, oil on canvas by J.W. Carmichael, 1841.

63. Durham Cathedral, West View, engraving after R.W. Billings, 1846.

64. Above the Rooftops, watercolour by Thomas Greenhalgh, 1884.

65. The Galilee, Evening, charcoal by Dennis Creffield, 1987.

66. The Central Tower, Durham Cathedral, charcoal by Dennis Creffield, 1987.

67. A Beam, charcoal by Virginia Bodman, 1983.

68. The Screen from the Triforium in the North Transept, watercolour by Birtley Aris, 1987.

69. The Screen and Choir from the North Transept Clerestory, watercolour by Birtley Aris, 1988.

70. Kathedra, sandstone sculpture by Colin Wilbourn, 1988.

71. Cuthbert of Farne, wooden sculpture by Fenwick Lawson, 1983

72. William of St. Calais, Ms B.II 13, 11th century commentary on psalms.

73. Hugh of le Puiset, Ms A.II.1, 12th century, David mourning over Saul and Jonathan.

Acknowledgements

The City of Durham Trust was founded in 1942 on the initiative of Dr. Cyril Alington, Dean of Durham. On the 900th anniversary of the cathedral, it was therefore fitting that the Trust should reciprocate with a celebratory volume on the famous building, and that the present Dean, Dr. John Arnold, should provide the Foreword. The print run of that volume was soon exhausted. Now, two years later, the millenium of the arrival of the St. Cuthbert Community and the founding of the see of Durham provide the opportunity for a second edition, which has been revised to incorporate a chapter on the saint in whose honour the cathedral was erected.

As editor of the volume, I would like to thank the Dean for his second enthusiastic endorsement of the work and my fellow contributors for the alacrity with which they agreed to join the project, and for agreeing to donate profit from the sales of the volume to the upkeep of the building they love. Like-minded generosity is also acknowledged to the following organisations for waiving or reducing the charge for reproduction of works of art in their collections: Trustees of the British Museum; Courtauld Institute of Art (Witt Gallery and Conservation of Wall Painting Department); Royal Academy of Art; Tate Gallery; Victoria and Albert Museum; the National Gallery of Scotland; Laing Gallery, Newcastle-upon-Tyne (Tyne and Wear Museums); Castle Museum, Norwich; Bildarchiv Preussischer Kulturbesitz, Berlin; and, of course, the Dean and Chapter Library, Durham.

The source of each particular work of art is recorded in the catalogue at the back of the volume. Plates II, III and IV and Figs. 43-48 are Crown Copyright. Douglas Pocock supplied the cover photograph and Figs. 2-6; the expert camera of Malcolm Thurlby provided Plates I and V and Figs. 11-26, 28-34. Michelle Johnson was responsible for all of the preparatory photographic work. Much of the text was typed by Edith Pocock; the design layout was by Arthur Corner and David Hume of the Cartographic Unit, University of Durham.

Foreword

Durham Cathedral is one of those rare works of art which go on inspiring other works of art. It is as if the creative forces which first went into this great construction could not be contained within it but must continually be overflowing, like the streams of living water which Ezekiel saw issuing from the Temple.

The ninth centenary of the laying of the foundation stones in 1993 led many people in the locality and further afield to respond imaginatively to what is after all only a conventional chronological marker. We had the feeling that they were only waiting for an opportunity to express their appreciation and, more than their appreciation, their love of 'the best building in the world', for Durham Cathedral inspires affection as well as amazement and awe.

These are the emotions which Douglas Pocock and his fellow symposiasts convey. Their work is rightly called 'a celebration'. For all the meticulous and well researched scholarship, this is no dry-as-dust architectural history or aesthetic analysis. The quality of enjoyment keeps on breaking through the necessary disciplines of authorship just as, incidentally, it does for those of us who are privileged to worship daily in this wonderful place. It plays its part in the transmission of the faith which raised 'this sumptuous church' and which sustains it still.

I am glad that a second edition should be called for on the eve of our celebration of the millenium of the foundation of the first Anglo-Saxon cathedral here in 995; and I am happy to commend it to you.

John Arnold.

Dean of Durham
23rd August 1994

7

1 St. Cuthbert and his Church

Douglas Pocock

The story of Durham Cathedral begins in AD 651 with the vision of St. Aidan being carried into heaven. The vision belonged to Cuthbert, a remarkable figure in British history.[1] His life was one of irony and paradox. He could be described, for instance, as a Scot trained in Irish spirituality who became head of England's most powerful religious house. Again, although a hermit or anchorite at heart, he was a contemplative who accepted roles as missionary pastor, monastic guestmaster, prior and bishop. And, not least, it is ironic that a man who for preference dwelt in a small wooden cell, should, four hundred years after his death, be the inspiration for the construction of one of the world's most remarkable buildings.

Cuthbert

Cuthbert's birth is broadly dated one year before the founding of the pioneering Christian community on the island of Lindisfarne by Aidan, brought from Iona in 635 at the invitation of King Oswald. It was his vision at the time of Aidan's death that drew Cuthbert, aged 17, to follow in the founder's footsteps. He entered the nearby daughter monastery of Melrose, rather than Lindisfarne, attracted by the reputation of an Irish monk, Boisil, from whom he absorbed the ways of Celtic spirituality. He eventually succeeded Boisil as prior, after a brief spell as guestmaster at Ripon, before becoming prior at the mother house on Lindisfarne. The momentous Synod of Whitby of 664 had just taken place. Here, after heated debate, the northern church agreed to accept the Roman Easter and abandon the Irish/Celtic calendar. Cuthbert's own life, in reconciling within himself both traditions, must have been influential in persuading fellow members of the community to fall into line with their southern brethren.

Cuthbert combined monastic administration with preaching and pastoral visiting away from Lindisfarne, but his heart was increasingly drawn to the contemplative life. After some ten years, therefore, he sought solitude, first, on a small island just off the main isle (known today as St. Cuthbert's Island), and then, about 676, with permission of his abbot and brothers, on the more distant Farne Island. Even here, however, his reputation for holiness and miracle-working meant that his solitude was far from unbroken. In 685, reluctantly but in obedience to King Ecgfrith and Archbishop Theodore, he was made Bishop of Lindisfarne. He travelled widely around his extensive diocese before resigning less than two years later through failing health. He spent Christmas 686 with his brothers on Lindisfarne, and then sailed to his Farne cell, a sick man seeking to spend his last days in prayer and solitude. He died on 20th March 687, and was buried, not in his cell, but beside the altar of the priory church.

St Cuthbert and his Community

Cuthbert was dead, but his reputation lived on, and however ascetic his earthly life might have been, in death he was honoured like an emperor.[2] Miracles continued to be worked at his tomb, and on the eleventh anniversary of this death in 698 he was proclaimed a saint. Affirmation of the canonization was given by the uncorrupt nature of his body when it was disinterred for translation to an elevated stone shrine. He was clothed in magnificent vestments and jewellery, including his pectoral cross. Further enrichment came with the sumptuously-illustrated *Lindisfarne Gospels* commissioned for the shrine by Bishop Eadfrith (698-721). The estimate that five hundred calves skins were required for its production, the earliest great masterpiece of English medieval book painting, is an indication of the monastery's wealth, in addition to the Community's desire to honour and proclaim their saint. A written record or testimony of the saint's life was also commissioned and produced by an anonymous Lindisfarne brother within two or three years of the enshrinement;[3] Bede soon followed with both a verse and prose life of Cuthbert, besides giving fuller treatment in his *Ecclesiastical History of the English People* in 831.[4] Wonder-working relics beside the shrine added a further important dimension to the emerging legend and 'cult' of St. Cuthbert. Notable were his chasuble and shoes, removed at the translation, and clippings of his hair. Even cut-up pieces of covering from his Farne oratory were attributed with miracle-working properties.

Within a century the priory church had been rededicated and the Community itself known after Cuthbert (and not the founding saint, Aidan). Cuthbert, in fact, is the clearest example in all Anglo-Saxon England of a saint's culture binding together and guaranteeing continuity of a community.[5] He was patron, as well as saint, seen as the guarantor through his continuing role as recipient and defender of the Community's lands and privileges.[6]

Possession of the body of their dead, yet still active, leader was of crucial significance. The fact that it was undecayed was God's sign of his servant's sanctity. (Inspections of the body after the initial enshrinement are recorded in 1104, on the saint's translation to the shrine in Durham; in 1537, at the dissolution, when its condition was presumably the reason for not destroying the valuable accompanying relics in the coffin; in 1829 and in 1899, when it was reported that a quantity of flesh was still adhering to the bones).[7] When the Community was forced to leave Lindisfarne in 875 under threat of Viking attacks, they naturally took the body with them, along with the relics and treasures. For seven years they were a peripatetic community, crossing to Cumbria and Galloway before recrossing the Pennines to North Yorkshire and eventually travelling north to Chester-le-Street in 882. Here, in a new church dedicated to St. Mary and St. Cuthbert, the body rested for more than a hundred years. (For a period the settlement was also known as Cuthbert's Town). In 995, under renewed Viking threat, the Community fled to Ripon, but after a few months they started on the return journey northwards, stopping seven miles short of Chester-le-Street at their new and final home of Durham (Fig. 2a).

Even during the period of wandering the saint remained active. He intervened, for instance, when the Community attempted to migrate to Ireland, his sign of displeasure being shown in waves from a previously calm sea crashing into the boat and turning to blood. He could also be judged instrumental in the choice of location of Chester-le-Street through his 'appearance' to Abbot Eadred. In the first vision Eadred was instructed to advise the Danes to elect Guthred as their king; in the second he was to request from Guthred extensive lands between the rivers Tyne and Tees. Chester-le-Street, clearly, was now optimally located with regard to the Community's territories compared with the peripheral position of Lindisfarne. The later choice of Durham is also attributed to St. Cuthbert, for when within a few miles of Chester-le-Street, to which the community was apparently returning in 995, the coffin became immoveable. It was released only after three days fasting and vigil, during which it was revealed to one of their number that their saint wished his home to be at nearby Durham. The wanderings, recorded in 11th century accounts - and in Scott's poem, 'Marmian' - give few details of their exact itinerary, but there seems little doubt that they may be interpreted within the context of the Community's estates and holdings, which were found as far north as the Forth, west at Carlisle and Cartmel and south as far as York (Fig. 2b). Such extensive holdings were the result of royal, as much as saintly, patronage. The early history of the Community was

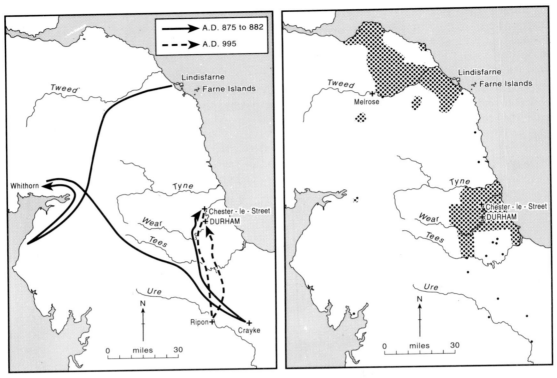

Fig. 2 (a) Wanderings of St. Cuthbert Community, (b) Lands, estates, houses sometime attached to the Community

intertwined with the Bernician power base at nearby Bamburgh and the emergence of Northumbria as the most powerful kingdom in the country, extending from the Humber to the Forth. Its subsequent, more complex, history was linked to Northumbrian, Danish, Saxon, even Scottish, royalty, either directly by pilgrimage and gifts or through the intervention of the saint in visions. A political interpretation may also be given alongside that of the saint's part in the choice of Durham, for it was not without significance that the leader of the St. Cuthbert Congregation in 995, Bishop Aldhun, had as a son-in-law, Uhtred, the rising earl of Northumbria. Uhtred certainly shared in making the peninsula at Durham suitable for settlement; he had also fortified the strategic site sufficiently to repel a Scottish army soon afterwards.[8] (Thus, the story which began on Lindisfarne or Holy Island, concluded on Dunholm or 'hill-island', the appropriate name for the raised plateau within the meander loop of the river Wear).

St. Cuthbert at Durham

Having acceded to the saint's wish to rest at Durham, the Community quickly established themselves in their headquarters. For the first time in their history, Cuthbert's shrine was enclosed in a stone church, an impressive twin-towered building completed in 1017. In 1022 the bones of Bede were brought from Jarrow to add to the wealth of relics. Royalty continued to be attracted, not least Cnut in 1031, who added to the Community's land in the south of the emerging county and bishopric. (It is interesting to note that for some time the inhabitants on the estates of St. Cuthbert between the Tyne and Tees had been known as 'haliwerfok', O.E.

for 'folk of the holy man', and that by association the title came to refer to the land itself, so that had the move to Durham not occurred, the name of the present county might well have indicated that it was indeed the land of Cuthbert's people).

Renewed political upheaval occasioned by the Norman invasion in the second half of the 11th century brought an initial brief flight back to Lindisfarne (1069-70), but subsequent relationships with the country's new rulers meant that the Community of St. Cuthbert emerged with enhanced prestige, although it was to undergo a transformation no less profound than that of the Celtic-Roman encounter four centuries earlier. William the Conqueror confirmed the lands, laws and liberties of the Church and installed the first in a line on non-hereditary bishops in 1071. A year later the king furnished the bishop with a stone castle, which was also the episcopal palace. In 1093 the second Norman bishop, William of St. Calais, ordered a replacement of the existing cathedral. Nine years earlier he had reformed the Community into a celibate, monastic order by bringing Benedictine monks from the recently re-founded Jarrow and Monkwearmouth houses. (The Congregation of St. Cuthbert had evolved over time into a mixed community, partly of monks, partly of secular and married clergy).

Confirmation of the continued privileged nature of the Community came at the enshrinement of Cuthbert in the new cathedral in 1104 when the body was inspected and found still to be undecayed. Certification was provided by Symeon's *History of the Church at Durham*,[9] a work by a resident monk which, in devoting three-quarters of its text to Cuthbert and history of the Lindisfarne Community, intentionally emphasized tradition and continuity. The succession of Durham to the Lindisfarne inheritance was also writ in stone when the island's ruined priory was rebuilt with pillars and vaulting echoing those of the new mother church (see Fig. 31).

The abbey church and its abbey functioned for another four centuries until the dissolution, when the monastic community was eventually transformed into the dean and chapter of the cathedral. The latter building itself was stripped of its Cuthbert designation and of the elaborate shrine of the saint, together with other embellishments. Otherwise, the buildings of abbey and church were left largely intact, so that the history to which they bear witness may be readily unlocked by the modern pilgrim, whether architect or artist, scholar or tourist. It is to the cathedral, however, as one of the most remarkable buildings in the world, that attention most naturally focuses.

St. Cuthbert's Cathedral

The cathedral erected at Durham to house the shrine of St Cuthbert is not only a cultural benchmark, but also an aesthetic high and an architectural innovation.[10] All three qualities were cited when it was designated a World Heritage Site in 1987.

In architectural terms, Durham Cathedral is where the structural thrust problem in major buildings was resolved, where the buttress, rib-vault and pointed arch of the Gothic were first demonstrated, albeit in a Romanesque, or Norman, construction. The achievement, according to Pevsner in his *Outline of European Architecture,* represented "the ultimate fulfilment of that tendency towards articulation which had driven Romanesque architects forward for over a hundred years".[11] The architectural, or engineering, achievement was an international one, with the skill and imagination of William of St. Calais and his Norman builders bringing to fruition the accumulated wisdom from contacts further afield in southern Europe - with

Fig. 3 View from Observatory Field

Fig. 4 View from Railway Station

Fig. 5 **View** from below Prebends' Bridge

Fig. 6 **View** from below Framwellgate Bridge

ecclesiastical buildings in Lombardy and with Islamic work in Spain. But it was at Durham that the vision was realised.

The speed of construction was remarkable, with the whole building being completed within forty years of laying the foundation stone in 1093. Building material was near to hand, initially cut stone from the dismantling of the recently erected Saxon cathedral, and then from quarries on the sides of the river gorge and from just beyond the west bank. Uniformity of material, allied to speed of erection - and restraint in subsequent restorations - has produced a building of remarkable purity: in fact, the most perfect example of late Romanesque. In context it represents the supreme architectural creation of a period when this country was at the forefront of European art in general.[12] As a consequence, the cathedral of Durham is a building by which others are judged and a place of pilgrimage for any serious student of architecture.

Durham is doubly noteworthy in that its innovative architectural features are housed in a remarkable building in a dramatic setting. Engineering achievement is combined with aesthetic quality. The standard two-volume work on Byzantine and Romanesque architecture by Jackson, for instance, describes the stature of the cathedral in the following terms:

> "The exterior of Durham, with its three massive towers, its enormous bulk, and its superb position on a rocky promontory round which the River Wear sweeps in a grand wooded defile, makes perhaps the most impressive picture of any cathedral in Europe".[13]

The aesthetic attraction is evident for all to see, with the interplay of building, site and setting producing a surprising variety of scenic views (Figs. 3-6), whether at close quarters, middle or long distance.[14] It is the view of the cathedral in its setting that caused medieval travellers to liken Durham to Jerusalem, Ruskin in the last century to proclaim it as one of the wonders of the world and Pevsner more recently to pronounce it as one of the architectural experiences of Europe.

Innovative architecture in a dramatic setting celebrates a cultural happening. In housing the shrine of St. Cuthbert, the building is witness to the role played by the saint in the spread of Christianity in northern England, a role equivalent to that played by St. Augustine in the south. And since the Anglo-Saxon cathedral protecting the shrine was replaced by a massive Romanesque temple, it is witness also to the Norman Conquest of England, symbol of the new Latin civilisation brought by the last invaders of this country.

Conclusion

The ultimate distinctiveness of Durham Cathedral stems from the fact that it witnesses to a story: that architecture and aesthetics point to the Norman confirmation of an earlier history and Saxon saint. The existing Norman structure represents time locked-up, a gigantic pause in the temporal flow of history. At the same time, in Eliot's phrase, one is aware in Durham of the presence, as well as the pastness of the past, for the story is kept alive, celebrated, enacted daily, weekly, annually by its clerics along with citizens, scholars, miners and a host of other regional and diocesan groups, as well as by modern pilgrims. Accordingly, this celebratory volume is to be seen as part of this ongoing process as the authors of subsequent chapters share with the reader their appreciation of one of the most outstanding buildings in the world.

2 The Building of the Cathedral: the Romanesque and Early Gothic Fabric

Malcolm Thurlby

Introduction

The Romanesque cathedral of St Cuthbert at Durham, which was erected between 1093 and 1133, is one of the most celebrated edifices of its age not just in terms of English architecture but in a truly European sense. It is conceived on a monumental scale that rivalled works such as the imperial cathedral at Speyer (commenced 1030, nave and transepts rib-vaulted after 1083), the third abbey church at Cluny (commenced 1088), and a number of Anglo-Norman churches starting with the great Benedictine abbey church of St Albans (commenced 1077). Durham is probably the earliest church in Europe to be vaulted throughout with rib-vaults,[1] a motif that was to evolve as one of the hallmarks of Gothic architecture. Of course, the emphasis on mural mass and surface in Durham is entirely Romanesque, but Durham is often seen in a proto-Gothic context because the nave high rib-vault has pointed transverse arches, and it has been argued that the quadrant arches across the galleries transfer the thrust of this high vault to the aisle walls in a way that presages the Gothic flying buttress.[2] Whilst a direct lineage between these motifs at Durham and their developed French Gothic counterparts is most unlikely, Durham was not without influence in the north of France and Normandy in the 12th-century. But more importantly, the rich articulation and delight in surface pattern in Durham Cathedral sets the standard for ecclesiastical architecture in Britain down to the 14th-century. Durham created an aesthetic which fused Anglo-Saxon surface enrichment with the logical articulation of Norman design on a scale that spoke of the power of the new rulers of England. How this new aesthetic was devised is one of the questions we have to address by trying to ascertain the roles of the patron(s) and the master mason(s) in the design process. In so doing we examine the iconography of the cathedral, and consider where the first master mason might have been trained. There are no written records to assist in this quest; our assessment is made through a sleuth-like reading of the fabric in search of vital clues.

Documentation[3]

The monastic buildings begun by Bishop Walcher (1071-1080) are probably those in the centre of the east range to the south of the chapter house.[4] Between 1088 and 1091, during the exile of Bishop William of Saint-Calais (1081-1096), the monks built the refectory and probably the west side of the Deanery undercroft. The refectory undercroft does not occupy the full length of the south cloister walk but was constructed in connection with the west wall of the first cloister which has been excavated in line with the third buttress from the south-west corner of the present cloister.[5] The scale of the present cloister was devised with the Anglo-Norman cathedral and therefore plans for the latter had not crystallised when the refectory was built. In 1092 Bishop William ordered the demolition of the White (Anglo-Saxon) Church, and on 11 August 1093 he and Prior Turgot laid the foundation stones of a "fabric much larger and more noble, which he intended to erect." The monks built their own offices and "the bishop carried on the works of the church at his own expense."[6] After Bishop William's death in January 1096, the monks continued the work on the church and, according to Simeon's continuator,

Fig. 7 Longitudinal section of north side. (Plate I, Billings)

Fig. 8 Longitudinal section of north side. (Plate II, Billings)

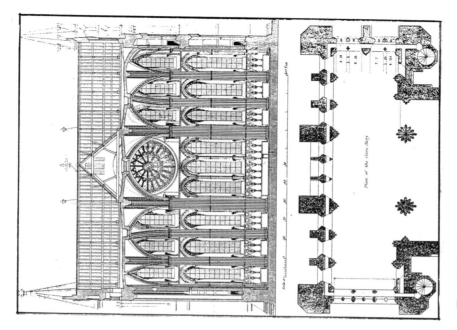

Fig. 10 Nine Altars : section to east, and plan. (Billings)

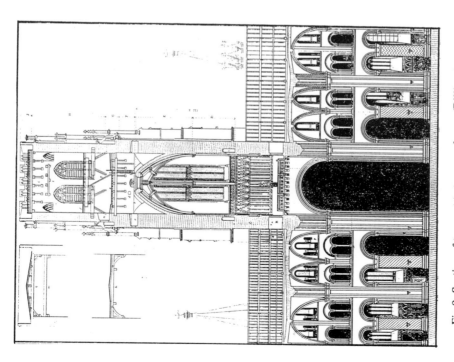

Fig.9 Section of transeot to tower and east. (Billings)

17

when Ranulf Flambard was appointed bishop in 1099 the building had advanced as far as the nave. This probably means that no more than the lowest courses of the nave aisle walls had been built for it is unlikely that the full elevation of the choir, transepts and first bays of the nave could have been achieved in so short a time. During Flambard's episcopate (1099-1128) work progressed *modo intentius, modo remissius*. In 1104 the body of St Cuthbert was translated from the White Church to its new resting place behind the high altar. At this time the eastern arm of the cathedral would have been complete. Work was finished by 1128 with the exception of the nave vault and the superstructure of the western towers. The nave vault was erected by 1133 but the twin western towers were not finished until the early 13th-century.

The chapter house was constructed for Bishop Geoffrey Rufus (1133-1140). Bishop Hugh of le Puiset (1153-95) commenced an extension at the east end of the cathedral but it collapsed and work transferred to the west end where he built the Galilee Chapel. In 1242 work began on the Chapel of the Nine Altars to replace the main apse and the easternmost bays of the Romanesque aisles.[7]

Discussion

The replacement of the Anglo-Saxon cathedral with the present building conforms to standard practice after the Conquest, as at Canterbury in 1070, Lincoln (1072/5), St Albans (1077), Winchester (1079), Ely (ca.1081) and so on. In each case the new Anglo-Norman church was conceived on a scale far grander than its predecessor and one that often revived the great Early Christian basilicas of 4th-century Rome.[8] At Durham the length of the 1093 church was based on Old St Peter's in Rome, a fitting parallel for the new house of the shrine of St Cuthbert (Figs. 1, 7-10. These figures should be consulted throughout this chapter). The scale analogue is not a new one for post-Conquest England; St Albans, Winchester and Ely cathedrals were all created in this grand manner and in each case they housed an important local saint as at Durham. All four buildings had four-bay eastern arms, an element unparalleled in churches in Normandy. Winchester may also provide the source for a number of motifs at Durham: the alternation of major and minor piers in the main arcades, the interior aisle wall dado arcade, the stepped shafts of the aisle vault responds, and even a rudimentary forerunner of the shafts behind the columnar pier. But Durham surpassed Winchester in decorative richness and articulation. The aisle dado arcades at Durham have moulded intersecting arches rather than plain round-headed arches at Winchester (Plate I). The main arcade and gallery arches at Winchester are unmoulded (Fig. 11); those at Durham have angle roll and hollow mouldings and large soffit rolls that give great plasticity to the arches (Fig. 12). Similarly, plain cylindrical piers at Winchester are given incised patterns at Durham, a translation into sculptured form of painted columns that can still be seen, for example, at Saint-Pierre at Chauvigny (Vienne). The same principle is witnessed in the introduction of the rib into the vault as a three-dimensional version of the painted groin of the type still extant in the presbytery aisles at St Albans. Whilst at Winchester the side shafts of the stepped aisle responds carry the groins, at Durham the articulation of the aisle bays is given full plastic expression through the ribs and moulded transverse arches linking the stepped shafts behind the main arcade piers with those of the responds (Fig. 13). Thus each shaft and capital carries its own arched element in a logical manner that evolves from Winchester and ultimately from Norman works like William the Conqueror's church of St Etienne at Caen.

Fig. 11 Winchester Cathedral, north transept looking N W

Fig. 12 Presbytery, looking S E

Fig. 13 Vault of North Presbytery aisle, looking west

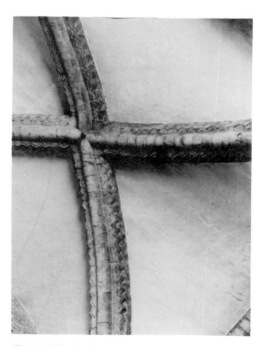

Fig. 14 Vault of fifth bay from crossing in nave south aisle

Fig. 15 Remains of wooden centring boards, nave south gallery

Fig. 16 Fragment of Romanesque vault web between Frosterly Marble shaft and Gothic vault web, south presbytery

Fig. 17 South presbytery gallery, looking east

According to 19th-century rationalist theory the rib served a structural purpose by reinforcing the groin of the vault through which it was believed the major forces were channelled to the corners of the bay.[9] However, the computer-assisted research of Robert Mark has demonstrated that the forces with rib and groin-vaults are not first directed to the groin or rib and then to the corner of the bay, but that they funnel equally through the vault web towards the corners.[10] Whether the medieval architect knew this is another matter, but at least the continued use of groin-vault long after the introduction of the rib - especially in undercrofts where stability for the superstructure would be of paramount importance (e.g. in the dormitory undercroft at Kirkstall Abbey) - suggests that the rib-vault was not perceived as structurally superior to the groin-vault.

The rib did assist in the creation of truer diagonals within the vault, but the serpentine movement of some ribs at Durham indicates that the ribs were laid up with the vault web rather than being constructed in advance of the web (Fig. 14).[11] In other words, the Durham vaults were constructed in the same way as groin-vaults. Complete wooden formwork was erected in each bay onto which the cut-stone ribs and rubble webbing were laid in mortar. When the whole was set, the formwork could be dismantled and moved to the next bay. The undertaking was a more complex version of the wooden centring for arches, some planks of which are still in situ in the enclosing arches in the nave galleries (Fig. 15). Bilson tells us that in the nave high vault "between the tops of the ogives (diagonals) and doubleaux (transversals) there is always a wide joint (of 2 inches or so) which received the boards of the centring on which the cells were built, and some fragments of oak boards were found in the course of repairs."[12] There are no such gaps in the choir and transept vaults, and throughout the church the ploughshared sections of the webs could only have been constructed on full centring which also cradled the ribs.

Dado arcades are used on the exterior walls of the cathedral except in the cloister. Those on the north side were recut in the 1780s but the original form is still preserved on the south side of the choir. The apse of Saint-Nicholas at Caen provides a parallel for these arcades, but in general the concept of the rich surface decoration may have come from Anglo-Saxon buildings.[13] Whilst the intersecting arches of the internal dado arcade are not preserved in an Anglo-Saxon building, the motif can be traced back to the eighth century in the Canon tables of Insular manuscripts, as in the Canterbury Bible (London, British Library, Royal Ms. I.E.VI). The tall moulded plinths of the exterior walls and the main arcade piers find conceptual parallel in such pre-conquest works as the chancel at Repton (Derbyshire) and the porticus entrance arch responds at Hadstock (Essex). The high-vault shafts on the gallery sills of the choir and transepts introduce articulation at first-storey level in the manner of the upper external arcades on the chancel at Bradford-on-Avon (Wilts) where triple and quintuple shaft groups are created from single stones in the same way as the paired shafts of the Durham internal dado arcades. The crypt at Repton also provides a parallel for the spiral columns, albeit on a far smaller scale. Whether or not this last feature represents an element of Anglo-Saxon continuity after the Conquest, there can be no doubt that the iconographic reference is to St Peter's shrine in Rome.[14]

The three-storey elevation comprising main arcade with alternating major compound and minor cylindrical piers, gallery and clerestory may drive from Winchester presbytery[7], although the proportions of the tall main arcade and squat gallery at Durham are more closely presaged at St Albans. Romanesque St Albans also had a high groin-vault over the presbytery

Fig. 18 North transept, looking N W

Fig. 19 North transept from south nave gallery

Fig. 20 North transept, looking S E

Fig. 21 North transept / north respond of east
crossing arch from south presbytery gallery

Fig.22 Coursing of SE high-vault capital, with east respond of north crossing arch, north transept

Fig.23 Springer of high vault over bays 1 and 2 in east gallery, north transept

which provides a precedent for the vaulted presbytery at Durham.[15] The Romanesque presbytery high vault at Durham was replaced with the present vault during the addition of the Chapel of the Nine Altars, but the form of the Romanesque vault can be reconstructed with some certainty. From the major piers the transverse and diagonal ribs of the Gothic vault spring from the three Romanesque shafts that rise from the ground (Figs. 7, 12). At gallery level these are flanked by Romanesque shafts surmounted by Gothic Frosterley marble shafts with stiff-leaf capitals which carry the wall arch of the vault. Adjacent to the Frosterley shafts the scars of the original vault are clear. They arc up to the apex of the clerestorey window but not beyond. This apparent asymmetry reflects the design of the Gothic vault rather than the Romanesque original. Above the minor piers the three Romanesque shafts set on the gallery sill carry the transverse and diagonal ribs of the Gothic vault. There are no Romanesque shafts to carry the Frosterley shafts and the Gothic wall arch, and therefore the Frosterley shafts are set on corbels. These shafts mask the traces of the Romanesque vault, but the erection of scaffolding in 1991 to clean the high vault afforded the opportunity for close examination behind the Frosterley shafts. In all cases the trace of the Romanesque vault was visible and in one case fragments of the Romanesque rubble web were still in place (Fig.16). This evidence

Fig.24 Bays 1 and 2 of east side of south
transept

Fig.25 Bays 3 and 4 of east side of south
transept

demonstrated that the trajectory of the Romanesque vault above the minor piers mirrored that above the major piers. These symmetrical lunettes accord with quadripartite rib-vaults over single bays with transverse ribs above the minor piers and transverse arches above the central stepped triplet of the major piers. As in the aisles, there is a one-to-one correspondence between the arched elements in the vault and their shafts.

The erection of a stone vault over the main span of the presbytery presented problems of stability. It has been suggested that the diaphragm arches behind the gallery piers provided abutment for the high vault (Fig. 17).[16] However, had the diaphragm arches been intended for a buttressing function then the stonework above them would have continued behind the springing of the high vault. As it does not, then we must conclude that the diaphragm arches were used in connection with the roof structure over the gallery. The thrust of the high vault was therefore absorbed within the seven-foot thick wall.

The pitch of the presbytery gallery roofs is not original because the sill of the Romanesque clerestory windows extends below the top of the present roof. A straight line between the

Romanesque sills and the outer walls would not clear the tops of the diaphragm arches. It is therefore likely that there were gablets over the projecting sections of the diaphragm arches.[17]

Against the outer walls of the galleries at the chord of the Romanesque aisle apses spiral staircases start upwards. It has been suggested that these would have risen up as turrets.[18] As such they would not have given access to any other part of the building, in contrast to the turrets at Peterborough Cathedral which surmount staircases on the inner angles of the apse chord and provide a link between the gallery and clerestory. Therefore, it seems more likely that these Durham staircases were connected with towers over the square enclosed apses. This reading is supported by fragments of Romanesque ashlar on the gutteral wall above the apse chord diaphragm arches, and on the north side by a break in the coursing of the stonework on the corresponding clerestory buttress. This break is explained by the removal of the west wall of the tower when the 13th-century extension of the presbytery was built. Eastern towers were used in the Romanesque fabric of Hereford Cathedral, and possibly at Winchester, and seem to derive from Lotharingia where they were appeared before 942 at St Maximin at Trier.

The transept arms present a number of anomalies. Four highly articulated bays on the east contrast with three relatively plain bays on the west. Massive stair turrets project from the outer western angles both on the exterior and into the interior space (Fig. 18). The arches of the eastern bays diminish in scale from the crossing outwards, and the details of the clerestories and the ribs of the high vaults are different north and south. How are these anomalies to be explained?

The projecting stair turrets house spiral stairs 67 inches wide. This width is most unusual in the context of major Anglo-Norman churches in which staircases are generally about three feet wide. One important exception is the main staircase in Remigius's westblock at Lincoln Cathedral which is 58 inches wide. The Lincoln westblock was conceived as a fortified structure, and it is in castle keeps that parallels for the Durham stairs are found. The closest in form to Durham - especially to the stair turrets in the western towers - is Castle Hedingham (Essex) which is 60 inches wide and is set in a turret that projects into the interior space. This analogy, along with the multi-towered plan and the massively thick walls, suggests that the cathedral was designed in concert with the fortifications of the peninsula.[19]

The four bays on the east side of each transept provide three separate chapels in the eastern aisle and access to the choir aisles. The scale of the arch next the crossing was determined by the choir aisle, whilst each transept arm was generated in plan by doubling the square of the crossing. The first square extends from the centre of the crossing pier to the centre of the major pier of the east arcade and its west wall respond; the second from the centre of the major pier to the outer face of the stair turret. It seems strange that the outer face of the turret was aligned with the outer line of the square, unless it was in response to the south transept where the south wall may have been built adjacent to the north wall of the Anglo-Saxon church. At any rate this geometry results in the second bay on the east side occupying the space left between the arch to the choir aisle and the major transept pier, whilst the two outer bays are reduced in scale because the outward projection of the stair-turret and the thickness of the transept terminal are set within the square planning module. With this reduction of space it is not surprising that the length of the major pier in each transept is significantly less than in the presbytery; the use of the presbytery-scaled pier would have left insufficient room for entrance to the chapels. A concomitant of this pared-down length is the reduction of the vault shafts above the minor piers from three in the presbytery to two in the transepts (Figs. 12, 19). This is reflected in the high vault with two diagonal ribs springing from the shafts between bays one and two with no transversal. The outer bays are covered with a single quadripartite vault, and therefore the shafts between the third and fourth bays on the east simply continue up the wall surface to the web of the vault, like the shaft on the west wall of the main crypt at Christchurch Priory (Hants). Such apparent lack of logic in the articulation may suggest that the transept vaults were not conceived at the outset.[20] There is indeed evidence in the south arm for the erection of a wooden roof before the introduction of the present vault, but in the north transept the evidence speaks unequivocally of the intention to vault from the first. The shaft in the north-east angle of the north transept that carries the wall arch of the high vault rises from the floor and courses with the Romanesque stonework of the main arcade and gallery throughout its length. That the capital and abacus here range with the capital and abacus carrying the high-vault rib can only mean that the high vault is integral with the initial plan. This is confirmed by the shaft carrying the south-east diagonal rib of the high vault in the north transept which is set on the gallery sill next to the north-east crossing pier in exactly the

Fig. 26 Nave, north aisle, looking east

26

same way as the analogous shafts at the west end of the presbytery where they carried the diagonals of the high vault (Figs. 20, 21). And just as in the presbytery this transept shaft, complete with its capital and abacus, courses perfectly with the adjacent stonework (Fig. 22). The masonry to either side of the ribs in the spandrel between gallery bays 1 and 2 of the north transept is set at different levels; this could only occur if the ribs were built with the wall (Fig. 23). Finally, the clerestory passages behind the vault springers are just 7 feet 6 inches in height in order to provide a mass of masonry behind the springing of the high vault to act as abutment.

The high-vault ribs spring from the west wall of the north transept not from capitals atop sill-set shafts, but from corbels. The reason for their use is not hard to find. The first storey for their use is not hard to find. The first storey of the west wall has a triforium passage rather than a gallery as on the east side. Had the front plane of the triforium been set back 13 inches in the manner of the gallery, the passage would have been reduced to just 12 inches in width and thereby rendered useless as the means of access from the north-west stair turret to the north nave gallery.

The evidence in the south transept does not speak with the singularity of intention to vault witnessed in the north transept. On the east side of the south transept the arrangement up to the springing of the gallery arches is the same as in the north. Above this there are clear indications that the vault was an insertion. The capital next the crossing that carries the diagonal rib of the high vault is set higher than the crossing capitals, whilst the vault capitals between the first and second bays are clumsily placed (Fig. 24). The south-easternmost shaft intended for the wall arch as in the north transept carries the south-east high-vault rib, whilst the shaft intended for this job rises to the webbing of the vault (Fig. 25). Most importantly on both the east and west clerestories there are former openings that were blocked to allow the construction of the high vault. These openings were constructed in connection with a wood roof which preceded the present high vault. In this scheme the clerestory passage was 11 feet in height, as opposed to the 7 feet 6 inches of the north transept, because there was no need of the abutment afforded by the masonry above the lower passage. The ribs are ornamented with chevron as in the nave rather than the roll and flanking hollows in the north transept which go with the choir aisles.

If the north transept was built as planned with the high vault, whilst the wood roof constructed over the south transept represented a change in plan, the implication is that the north transept was built before the south. This would be unusual for a church with monastic buildings on the south side. However, delay in completing the south transept may have occurred if the terminal wall was contiguous with the Anglo-Saxon cathedral which remained in part until St Cuthbert was translated in 1104.[21]

Unlike the presbytery and transepts, the nave was not initially planned for a high vault. The front plane of the gallery is not set back from the main arcade, and the easternmost ribs of the high vault commandeer shafts that were originally intended for the outer order of the western crossing arch which is now rudely cut by the diagonals (Pl. V). The wood-roofed scheme was soon abandoned, however, and by the time the first clerestory bays were constructed the plan for the high vault was in hand. The stepped design of the clerestory inner plane follows the north transept, whilst the use of head corbels to carry the high vault ribs is continued from the west wall of the north transept. The chevron that adorns the high rib-vaults was introduced in

Fig. 27 Quadrant arches, before addition of two inner orders, nave south gallery (1843)

Fig. 28 Nave vault, looking east

the second major campaign of construction. Before discussing this campaign, certain differences must be noticed between the nave on the one hand and the choir and transepts on the other that were planned in the first great campaign. The nave aisles are wider than the choir aisles, the result of erecting the inner plane of the nave aisle wall in line with the out plane of the aisle wall in the choir. The minor piers of the nave arcade are 8-foot cylinders rather than 7-foot cylinders in the choir with attached shafts towards the aisle to carry the transverse arches and diagonal ribs of the aisle vault (Fig. 26). The nave aisle responds opposite the columnar piers are also demi-cylinders. In the first great campaign of construction two bays of the main arcade with the corresponding aisle vaults and one bay of the gallery were built on each side. Thus, the lozenge decoration on the first pair of columnar piers in the nave, rather than the spirals in the presbytery and transepts, was determined in phase 1, a continuation of the decorative variety already introduced in the chevron column in the south transept main arcade. With the resumption of work in phase 2, chevron is introduced in the arcade, gallery and clerestory arches, the doorways, as well as the vault ribs and the second pair of columnar piers. Whether or not this is the earliest chevron in England, it sets the standard for the shrine-like enrichment of churches in Britain through the remainder of the 12th-century. Further diversity comes with the flutes on the third pair of columnar piers. The inner faces of the north and south doorways are also encrusted with sculpture; there are foliated and figurated cushion capitals, and figurated medallions on the hood moulds, and on the shafts of the north doorway.

As in the presbytery, the erection of the high vault over the nave has led to discussion of abutment and in particular to the interpretation of the quadrant arches over the nave galleries as proto-flying buttresses (Fig. 27). But just as the diaphragm arches in the presbytery galleries were built in connection with the roof, so were the nave quadrant arches. A series of transverse gables covered the nave galleries, traces of which are seen in Billings's drawing of the south elevation before its restoration in 1850, and are still to be seen in certain bays on the north side.

There has been much ado about the introduction of pointed transverse arches in the nave high vault, another feature that is supposed to presage Gothic (Fig. 28). It is true that the pointed form does avoid the stilting evident in the round-headed transverse arches in the transepts, but it does little to transfer the thrust of the vault more closely to the vertical of the supporting walls and therefore seems to present little in the way of structural advance.

The core of the north doorway to the cathedral remains from the Romanesque period but it has undergone considerable reworking since its construction in the 1120s. The present frame of the doorway is the result of the "improvements" of the 1780s. Pre-restoration engravings show that there was a two-storey early Gothic porch, the foundations of which have been excavated recently. This took the place of a two-storey Romanesque porch, the evidence for which is a flight of stairs leading to the first storey of the porch from the gallery, and two small windows, now blocked, on the inner face of the wall above the doorway. The original was probably like the north porch at Kelso Abbey.

The twin-towered facade of Durham develops from Westminster Abbey and Canterbury Christchurch Cathedral and St Augustine's Abbey.[22] In all these examples the ground floor of the towers communicated with the western bay of the nave through full height main arcade arches, and is similarly open to the aisles. This openness presages the developed French Gothic *facade harmonique* as at Reims Cathedral. The inclusion of the towers involved a modification of the design principles elsewhere in the nave. The alternating system of compound and columnar piers is abandoned to provide massive piers strong enough to support towers. The tower bays are larger than the aisle bays and therefore the capital carrying the vault rib on each tower pier is set lower than the arcade capitals to avoid an unduly segmental trajectory of the rib.

Our appreciation of the Romanesque west front is diminished by the addition of the Galilee and the great west window, and by the late 18th-century chiselling back of the surface. But even if the detail cannot be trusted, at least the main lines of the design are clear. Pilaster buttresses express the internal division of nave and aisles, whilst the lowest three windows on the tower fronts correspond to aisle, gallery and clerestory. The two lower storeys are framed by giant arches that originally rose uninterrupted through the two storeys, and the enclosing arch of the central section of the facade is still extant.

The chapter house was erected between 1133 and 1140 in the usual place south of the south transept from which it was separated by the barrel-vaulted slype. The walls of both the chapter house and slype have (restored) intersecting blind arcades in which dosserets and shafts are created from monoliths, a motif formerly used in the crypt at Lastingham and subsequently in the chapter house at Rievaulx Abbey. The doorway has a richly chevroned arch and inhabited capitals on the inside by the same sculptors as the north and south doorways of the church. The modern vault incorporates the original rib design with chevron flanking the earliest keeled rolls in England.

The roles of patron and master mason in the design

The design of the cathedral would have been established through dialogue between patron, initially Bishop William, and mason. Concepts of scale, the number and placement of towers, the amount of decoration, and the inclusion of high vaults, would have originated with the patron. Thus parallels of size and iconography with St Peter's, Rome, would have been William's. His sense of rivalry with the new "shrine churches" of Winchester and St Albans would also have influenced the overall scale as well as the four-bay choir, the alternation of the main arcade piers, multiplication of towers and turrets, richness of decoration, and the high vaults. He would also have been aware of the compatibility of the design with the castle and the fortification of the peninsula. It is even possible that he asked the master mason to achieve the image of Anglo-Saxon setting for St Cuthbert.

Specific details would have come from the mason. Tynemouth Priory, which was commenced between 1085-1090, provides the immediate source for the plinths of the presbytery piers, the stepped shafted responds, columnar piers with octagonal capitals, cushion capitals, roll and hollow arch mouldings, and fine quality ashlar.[23] Similar responds also occur at Lastingham Priory (1078-1085) where the high groin-vault in the presbytery is an important precursor, albeit rebuilt, of the Durham rib-vaults.

The double-splay windows in the middle storey of the axial tower at Jarrow presage the original presbytery clerestory windows and the lowest window in the north transept stair turret at Durham. The intersecting arcades and chevron may have Islamic sources, but Anglo-Saxon precedents, not least in the art of church treasures, seem more appropriate for the decoration of the architectural shrine of St Cuthbert.[24] Thus in addition to the intersecting dado arcades in

Insular Canon tables, arches on the 8th-century Franks Casket (London, British Museum) introduce decorated shafts, multiple roll mouldings and chevron.

Galilee Chapel[25]

The Galilee was constructed at the west end of the cathedral by Bishop le Puiset after an abortive attempt to build an extension at the east end (Fig. 29). It has five aisles, each of four bays with round-headed arcades carried on slender quatrefoil piers with coursed limestone and dark marble shafts. The initial plan was for the paired marble shafts to stand alone, but the limestone shafts were soon added, thereby creating an image of greater stability. In the main the additional capitals and bases are carefully fitted to the originals, but in certain cases the new capitals have not been provided with abaci. The rich chevroned arches follow the design principle of the main church, but otherwise the mouldings are more delicate than the earlier work, not least the keeled rolls in the soffits and the waterleaf capitals. The emphasis on mural mass in the main church is here replaced with a sense of spaciousness which betrays a knowledge of developments in French Gothic architecture. This probably came through the choir of York Minster as rebuilt after 1154 by Archbishop Roger of Pont l'Eveque and perhaps the contemporary work in the cloister at Bridlington Priory. Affiliated work is seen at Newcastle Castle Chapel, in the hall (now chapel) at the Bishop's Palace at Bishop Auckland, in the north arcade at Hornby (N. Yorks), and elsewhere.

Chapel of the Nine Altars[26]

In 1235 Hugh Northwold, Bishop of Ely (1229-1252) granted an indulgence which offered thirty days remission to those contributing to the fabric fund of Durham where the vault over St Cuthbert's tomb was in imminent danger of collapse. At this time Bishop Richard Poore of Durham was planning to extend a new work at the east end of the church to provide a safer and more fitting place for Cuthbert. Work was started in 1242 and was completed about 1280. The general association of an eastern transept with a shrine is allied to Beverley Minster and Worcester Cathedral, but Durham was modelled directly on the Nine Altars at Fountains Abbey (commenced c. 1203-8). The free-standing piers at the entrance to the transept arms at Fountains are abandoned at Durham. However, other aspects of the plan are copied exactly, and this created alignment problems with the east and west vault responds, which contributed to the uncomfortable junctions between the transverse arches and the diagonal ribs in the bays next to the centre of the chapel.

The walls in the Chapel of the Nine Altars are seven feet thick as in the Romanesque fabric, and the richness of articulation and decoration follow similar principles even though the details are different. The dado arcade in the Nine Altars is much deeper and its spandrels are excavated with elongated quatrefoils (Fig. 30). Above this the wall is dissolved into a passage with tall lancet windows, and this is surmounted by a clerestory passage. The elevation follows closely the eastern extension at Tynemouth Priory which was erected to give a more magnificent setting for the shrine of St Oswin. The wall of the north front of the Nine Altars above the dado arcade is filled with a huge six-light bar-tracery window.[27] The mass of the responds is denied by the strong verticals of grouped limestone and marble shafts. Prolific stiff-leaf foliage sprouts from the capitals, and dog-tooth and other ornament encrust arches and vault ribs the way chevron embroidered these elements in the second phase of the

Fig. 30 Nine Altars Chapel, looking to north transept

Fig. 29 Galilee Chapel

Romanesque building. This rich decoration plus the use of marble allies the Nine Altars Chapel with shrine settings at Worcester and Ely cathedrals.

The extent to which the high vault of the Romanesque eastern arm was in danger of collapse in 1235 is difficult to determine. The documentation refers only to the vault above St Cuthbert's shrine, that is in the apse and forebay; perhaps settlement of the eastern towers may have contributed to the problem. Be that as it may, the high vault of the Romanesque presbytery was replaced with one aesthetically compatible with the Nine Altars to provide a vista of pointed arches east of the crossing and a successful visual transition between the Romanesque and Gothic sections of the cathedral.

Influence of Romanesque Durham

Romanesque Durham influenced the design of buildings from Orkney to northern France and Normandy. Lindisfarne Priory, a daughter house of Durham, was rib-vaulted throughout (Fig. 31). The alternation of compound and incised decorated columnar piers and corresponding compound and demi-cylindrical responds reflect Durham nave. The nave-vault shafts set on the gallery sill follows the presbytery and east side of the transepts at Durham, while the corbelled high vaults in the presbytery, crossing and transepts at Lindisfarne follow Durham transept west walls. The arch and rib mouldings are Durham-inspired and the west porch with upper-storey watching room probably reflects the north porch at Durham.

The nave of Selby Abbey has alternating major and minor piers and the first columnar pier of the south arcade has incised lozenge decoration (Fig. 32). The rib-vaults in the two eastern bays of the south nave aisle have Durham mouldings and at the back of the incised column they are carried on stepped shafts in the manner of the Durham choir aisles.

In the naves of Norwich Cathedral and Waltham Abbey are columnar piers with incised spirals like the Durham choir, and transept arcades appear, probably as liturgical markers for the nave altars, within an alternating system of piers. Decorated incised columns are also used in the alternating system in the nave of Kirkby Lonsdale (Cumbria), as an element in the nave piers at Lenton Priory and, after 1154, in the crypt piers of Archbishop Roger of Pont l'Eveque's York Minster.

At Dunfermline Abbey incised columnar piers are again used as liturgical markers, while all the arch mouldings, the rib-vaults and intersecting dado arcades of the nave aisles, and certain details of sculpture of the doorways are Durham-inspired (Fig. 33).[28] At Kirkwall Cathedral the rib-vaulted choir aisles, arch mouldings, intersecting dado arcades in the transepts and nave aisles, and the stair turrets jutting into the outer western angles of the transepts, all betray a detailed knowledge of Durham (Fig. 34).[29] Durham also influences the external blind arcades and grotesque corbels for rib-vaults in the parish churches at Dalmeny (Lothian) and Leuchars (Fife). On a different level, the vast scale of St Andrews Cathedral Priory, the location of the shrine of the patron saint, the transept plan with eastern aisles, and the rich arcaded decoration in the choir and transepts all reflect Durham.[30]

The rib-vaulted chancels at Warkworth, Heddon-on-the-Wall and formerly in Bamburgh Castle Chapel (Northumberland), have vault shafts set on a string course at the level of the window sill in the manner of the gallery sill-set shafts at Durham. Various details at Seaton

Fig. 31 Lindisfarne Priory, nave south
arcade

Fig. 32 Selby Abbey, nave south arcade

Fig. 33 Dunfermline Abbey, north
presbytery aisle

Fig. 34 Kirkwall Cathedral, north
presbytery aisle

34

Delaval and Old Bewick (Northumberland), and Corbridge, Heighington, Kirk Merrington (rebuilt 1850) and Lanchester (Co. Durham) all speak of Durham-trained masons.

The one grotesque head corbel remaining from the high vault added to the nave of Lincoln Cathedral by Bishop Alexander suggests the influence of Durham. More generally, the rib-vaults at Winchester Cathedral added after the 1107 fall of the tower, and those at Peterborough Cathedral commenced in 1118 may have been conceptually inspired by Durham.[31] The degree to which Durham influenced rib-vaulting in Normandy is difficult to determine, not least because the high rib-vault in the presbytery at Lessay was completed before the burial of Eudes au Capel there in 1098 and may even have been commenced before Durham.[32] Durham may be behind details like the grotesque corbels carrying the ribs at Tollevast and the aisle groins at Saint-Gabriel, but the influence does not appear to be direct. Later, the nave of Saint-Pierre at Lisieux has a recessed gallery with sill-set shafts interpreted from Durham.[33]

Certain details in the westblock of Abbot Suger's Saint Denis suggest Durham contact, including the lower setting of capitals taking diagonal ribs, and rich articulation of piers, responds and arches. Later *facade harmoniques*, like Reims Cathedral, ultimately reflect Durham.

Perhaps the most important aspect of Durham's influence, however, concerns the concept of a rich decorative aesthetic with the mutiplication of shafts on piers and mouldings in arches, and a wealth of applied ornament. This indulgence in linear pattern and surface encrustation continued into the early Gothic with Canterbury choir (1174-1184) and Glastonbury Abbey Lady Chapel (1184-1186), throughout the Early English of Lincoln Cathedral (1192-1280) and Ely Cathedral presbytery (1234-1252), to the richly textured thick walls of Decorated Exeter Cathedral (ca. 1270-1390) and Ely Cathedral Lady Chapel (ca. 1321-1349).[34]

Acknowledgement

I should like to thank The Dean and Chapter of Durham for permission to have total access to the cathedral. Mr Owen Rees, Head Verger, and Mr Reg Wright, Assistant Verger, have been models of helpfulness during my many visits. Mr Ian Curry, architect to the fabric of Durham Cathedral, has accompanied me over the building on numerous occasions, kindly gave permission to examine the choir high vault from scaffolding in 1991, and has freely shared his wealth of knowledge on the fabric. I have also benefitted from discussions with Dr Eric Cambridge, Ms Linda Denesiuk, Mr Stuart Harrison, Professor M.F. Hearn, Professor Lawrence Hoey, Mr Hugh McCague and most particularly with Professor Eric Fernie.

3 Continuity and Change: Masters, Surveyors and Architects to the Fabric of the Cathedral

Ian Curry

The Norman cathedral, rising from the rock of the peninsula, has foundations which gave the church an unmatched structural stability, while its superstructure was so well engineered that only one major change was needed when its eastern end was extended in the 13th-century. However, any historic building which remains in continuing and constant use is not a static monument, but a living structure subject to continuous adaptation and change. It is on the nature of the subsequent upkeep of the original Norman building, and on the authors of adaptation and change, that this chapter will focus.

The early Centuries

The names of the Norman Master Masons at Durham are not known, but a few names begin to emerge from the middle of the 12th century, when we have the names of two of the designers employed by Bishop Hugh of le Puiset - Richard de Wolveston (referred to as Ingeniator) who was probably responsible for the Galilee Chapel starting about 1170,[1] and followed by William and Engineer (also Ingeniator).

The most important alteration to the Norman building came in the middle of the 13th-century with the addition to the east end of the cathedral of an eastern transept, or Chapel of the Nine Altars, in place of the Norman apse, mainly to provide ample space round St Cuthbert's tomb for pilgrims. The high-vault of the quire was renewed at the same time, so that an extremely subtle harmony between the Romanesque and Early English work was achieved. This Chapel of the Nine Altars is a marvellous space, and such was its enrichment in mouldings and sculpture that it took as long to build as the whole Romanesque cathedral had done - forty years. Richard of Farnham was responsible for the new chapel; Thomas Moyses (c.1240) was also associated with the works, probably as mason.

In the 14th and 15th centuries we have the names of a handful of prominent Masters working at Durham. Roger the Mason was working on the Gatehouse Chapel in 1339 and probably inserted the Great West Window into the cathedral in 1341. John Lewyn was most important in the latter half of the 14th century, as master mason to the bishop, as well as working on some of the royal castles, for the Nevilles at Raby, and for John of Gaunt. He was designer of the new Priory Kitchen in 1368, and with its interlacing ribs to the octagonal vault, one is tempted to wonder what link there might have been with ideas from Spain, where John of Gaunt was claiming the Kingdom of Castile. Lewyn probably started the new cloisters at the end of the 14th century and may have designed the Hatfield monument (1362-1371), but was not responsible for the new tomb-base for St Cuthbert's Shrine or the Neville Screen (1371-1380), both of which were made in London workshops in the most up-to-date Court style, and may have been designed by Henry Yeveley. The masons John de Middleton in 1398 and Peter Dryng in 1401 contracted for the reconstruction of the Great Dormitory,[2] with Ellis Harpour as carpenter, and also John Dinsdale as mason. Peter Dryng undertook the tomb and chantry of

Bishop Skirlaw in 1402, while Thomas Hyndeley completed the cloisters between 1416 and 1430.

John Bell, Senior, worked on the infirmary from 1418 to 1429, and the Prior's Lodging from 1428 to 1432. In 1438, with William Chaumere, he inserted four new traceried windows into the quire, and two years later placed tracery in one of the nave windows. This, of course, was part of the process when all the main windows of the cathedral were either enlarged or had tracery inserted. In 1429 the central tower and its steeple suffered lightning damage and a fire, and it was repaired between 1430 and 1437 by John Bell, Senior. Of this earlier crossing tower we know very little other than it may have been carried up at much the same time as the western towers, and that there was decorative metalwork in its steeple. After a second fire in 1459 the tower was rebuilt between 1465 and 1475 to the designs of Thomas Barton from York. The belfry stage at Durham was completed by John Bell, Junior, starting in 1483 and continuing until towards the end of the century. The belfry had been prepared with internal squinch arches for large corner pinnacles such as most late mediaeval towers would have had, but at Durham these were never completed. We shall see how our 18th and 19th century architects sought to remedy this omission.

The 16th century brought the Dissolution of the Benedictine Monastery, but it was relatively gentle. The King's Commissioners had taken down the Shrine of St Cuthbert, but the throne, Neville Screen and Castel Clock survived, the latter moved from the crossing into the south transept. In the 1540s Chapter minutes mention the purchase of incense, and setting up the Great Pascal for Maundy Thursday, and it was not until the 1570s under a puritanical dean that the pascal was destroyed and much else besides.

After the Dissolution, the Dean and Chapter records begin to make occasional references to repairing the 'leades' of the cathedral roofs between 1541 and 1596, and also to work on rehanging the bells in the central tower, but no names of craftsmen are mentioned. Nor is the maker of the new marble high altar installed for Dean Hunt in 1626. The bells were recast "to a solemme tune of six notes" in 1631 by Umfrye Keyne[3] (to be recast by Christopher Hodson in 1693). In these early years of the 17th century, there was a positive interest in Durham of restoring furnishings and services to something like they were before the destructions of Elizabeth's reign, but the Civil War was to be disastrous for the cathedral. All the internal wooden furnishings which had survived the Reformation were damaged, firstly by the invading Scottish troops in 1640, and then finally destroyed by the Scottish prisoners from Dunbar in 1650. The lead-covered timber spires or 'great broaches' of the western towers (Fig. 35) also were taken down in the 1650s, their material being sold.

Restorations, 1660 to 1774

The first meeting of the Chapter after the Restoration, held on 3rd November 1660, recorded

> "That Whereas the fabric of the Church and Chapter House is Exceeding Ruinous, the Leads much decayed, the Windows almost totally broken, and noe seats in the Quire, but such as have been made since his Majesties happy Restoration ... ... Hospitalities, Residences, etc. are impossible to observe for the present by reason of Ruines of the Deanery and Prebendaryes houses and want of furniture and other accommodation ....."[4]

Two days later John Cosin was elected bishop, and the next day the Chapter recorded

> "That some workmen of several professions be employed to View and value the Delapidations of the Church, Chapter House, College, Schoole House, and all other buildings either to the Church in generall or to the Deane and prebendaries in particular, And that thereupon Care be taken for Repairacions, with all convienient speed ... And that for the present 10 trees be cutt down and brought to the College to be seasoned this winter for making Stalls and seats in the Quire next Spring".[5]

So it would seem the Chapter had planned the new stalls before Bishop Cosin's enthronement, though as completed they were to be very much in the style associated with him, richly mixing Gothic canopy-work with Renaissance and Jacobean elements. It was a style that had already been established before the Civil War by Cosin and his fellow prebendaries in some of the parish churches of County Durham. John Clement may have been the designer or carver in charge of the work in the cathedral,[6] and so convincingly mediaeval is the tabernacle-work, one suspects that fragments of the originals may have survived to provide models for the new work; rather more Renaissance detailing appears in the lofty font canopy, and the choir screen was to be almost Baroque. John Cosin always had the keenest interest in the pre-Reformation survivals at Durham, and both his pre-Civil War and post-Restoration works in and around Durham should be regarded as Gothic Survival rather than early Gothic Revival. In July 1661 the Dean and Chapter ordered a "fair double organ"[7] from George Dallam of the parish of St Andrew by the Wardrobe, London, and this was in use by the end of 1662. The splendid organ which eventually surmounted the choir screen was built between 1683 and 1686 by (Father) Bernard Smith.[8]

John Sudbury had been dean since 1662 and before his death in 1684 he had arranged for the old frater or Petty Canons Hall to be rebuilt as a library. With its fine bookcases and reading desks in the style of a college library, it still stands much as he intended. The deanery itself was still said to be "in great decay" but was partly rebuilt on its northern side by the early 1690's. John Bowes may have been Supervisor of Works or Clericus Operum to the Chapter at this time, and his is the first recorded name in the Chapter Minutes of what was to be a continuous line of men overseeing the work on the fabric of the cathedral. However, the title Clericus Operum does not appear in Minutes until 1720.[9] From this time on in the 18th century the Clericus Operum was to be constantly engaged on works about the cathedral and the College. Repaving of the quire in marble was started in 1729, and paving the rest of the cathedral in stone continued until 1738. The cloisters were repaired between 1763 and 1769 with Mr Hogg as Clericus Operum, and it must have been at this time that whatever survived of the 15th century tracery of the cloisters was replaced by the present plain intersecting and uncusped tracery, which looks far from authentic. The basic 15th century piers and buttresses of the cloisters survive, though repaired in the 19th and 20th centuries.

Revival and Improvements, 1774 to 1827

The last quarter of the 18th century saw the advent of Early Gothic Revival works, marking the second phase of cathedral restorations. The 18th century also saw a series of topographical illustrations. There are several engravings showing the appearance of the north front prior to 1770; the western towers without parapets, just as they had been left after the removal of the great broaches; the two-storeyed Gothic north porch, with the royal arms of Elizabeth I set above the Norman portal; the angle turrets of the north transept with pyramidal roofs; and the

Fig. 35 North front before 1660, with lead-covered spires on west towers

Fig. 36 North front, 1754, "with minerets" pencilled in by Thomas Wright, 1770

north-east turret of the Nine Altars lopped off at eaves level. It was the Forster and Mynde's 1754 view of the north front which Thomas Wright used in 1770 to depict proposed new pinnacles, or "Minerets" as he called them, on the west towers, central tower, and north end of the Nine Altars (Fig. 36). Already in 1770, then, some enlightened people were thinking the cathedral exterior needed embellishments.

By this time it must have been becoming evident to the Chapter that the fabric of the cathedral needed attention, and at Dean William Digby's first Great Chapter on 20 November 1777, it was "Agreed that Mr Wooler be Employed to Survey the Church, and to make an Estimate of the Expenses of Repairing and Beautifying it." [10] It would seem the Chapter was as much concerned with improving the appearance of the cathedral as repairing its fabric. John Wooler, a Newcastle surveyor and engineer, was assisted by a Mr Gibbons and George Nicholson. (The latter, an architect and mason who lived in Bow Lane, in Durham, had recently designed the new Prebends' Bridge, built 1772-75 to replace the previous one swept away in the Great Flood of 17 November 1771). Wooler seems to have reported verbally to members of the Chapter as the survey proceeded. His report was written at Durham, and set out the repairs needed to the fabric of the church, most of which came to be carried out over the succeeding years.[11] The four corner turrets and the eastern buttresses of the Chapel of the Nine Altars were reported as being in a bad way, and also the gable and turrets of the north transept. A rent or crack had been discovered along the south side of the nave vault, though he thought it was not recent. He drew attention to the very poor state of all the external masonry, and proposed that it be chipped or pared away to a depth of one, two, or three inches in order to remove the weathering and decayed surfaces. Work was needed on the stonework of many of the windows, on the parapets and buttresses of the central tower, and on the north porch where the upper part had pulled away from the main structure. Wooler recommended that the western towers be properly finished with pierced parapets, and that they and the central tower should have "ragged pinnacles" to relieve their massive appearance. He finished by calculating that it would take eight years for a team of forty men to complete the work at a cost of £9,000.

Thus we have in this 1777 Report the essence of the works on the fabric of the cathedral during the next twenty years - the destruction of the ancient north porch; the chiselling away and resurfacing of the masonry of the east, north and west fronts of the church; the reconstruction of the north gables and upper parts of the northern turrets to the Nine Altars Chapel and North Transept; and the addition of pinnacles to the central and western towers, the first of several schemes for 'finishing' the top of the central tower, which never had received the pinnacles intended by its mediaeval designers.

The Chapter records do not indicate in which order the works were carried out, but expenditure was authorised on the repairs from 1778 onwards. However in February 1779 Wooler presented his 'memorial' or specification for taking down and rebuilding the north gable of the Nine Altars, including the construction of the present octagonal north-west and north-east stone spires of the chapel. This work must have proceeded immediately, to be followed in later years by the remainder of the north side of the cathedral. The Chapter paid Wooler 30 guineas on July 1782 "for his trouble in viewing and reporting the state of the Church". The amount of the payment helps to confirm the view that Wooler had been brought in as the consultant, but that the day-to-day organisation and supervision of the repairs was left to the Clericus Operum, and to Nicholson. (Records suggest that Nicholson was acting both as 'College Architect' and 'Clerk of Works' to the Chapter by 1777).

Fig. 37 North front, as proposed, 1777, drawn by George Nicholson

Wooler had proposed to the Chapter in the 1777 report that Nicholson be employed to measure and draw proper plans and elevations of the cathedral, so as to assist in "designing and depicting" the proposed beautifications of the church. We can assume that these survey drawings were prepared, though the original drawings to not seem to have survived. However, the first edition of William Hutchinson's *History of Durham*, published in 1787, gives two plates showing the north and east elevations, prior to the repairs being started, the north elevation being inscribed "Durham Abbey from a Measurement by G. Nicholson, Arct". The east front is shown with its north-east turret still truncated, lead-covered spires to the south-east and south-west turrets, and flanking the rose window, an arrangement of the large central buttresses and their niches with statues very different from that which now exist. More important, two original pen-and-wash drawings by Nicholson survive in the library of the Society of Antiquaries of London giving the west front and north front 'as proposed'. They show the 'ragged pinnacles' on the central tower and western towers as proposed in Wooler's report, and also show the north porch virtually in its present form, as are the north turrets to the Nine Altars and north transept (Fig. 37).

Hutchinson, writing in 1787, draws particular attention to the recent chiselling of the north front, and to the north porch having been "rebuilt and highly ornamented".[12] Thus the porch had been reconstructed in its present form by 1787, and almost certainly under the direction of Nicholson. All the chiselling and re-dressing of the lower parts of the east front will have continued under Nicholson, until his death in 1793. He was succeeded by William Morpeth. That the Chapter appointed him as architect rather than clerk of works is significant, for it is clear that he soon established himself as a dominant character in the College. He remained in office until 1814.

In February 1794 Durham also received a new dean, James Cornwallis, later Earl Cornwallis, who was already Bishop of Lichfield and Coventry, and at the meeting on 26 September 1794, the Dean and Chapter "Agreed that Mr James Wyatt be wrote to, to come down to inspect the repairs to the Cathedral, and to Give a Plan on the future Repairs and Improvements." [13] James Wyatt, (1747-1813), had earlier been called in by Bishop Shute Barrington to remodel the gatehouse of Durham Castle, and at this time was at the height of his career. Whatever his detractors might have said, he was the most fashionable architect in the country, the undisputed master of the Gothic style. Wyatt in due course presented his report and proposals, his set of drawings dated September 1795 being preserved in the Chapter Library. If he made a written report, this has not survived, but his intentions are clear from the drawings.

Wyatt's drawings quite distinctly indicate that the Galilee Chapel was to be removed, not for bringing a carriage drive round the church as is popularly supposed, but to allow the great west door to be re-opened. It was to be given a new outer porch, or rather the recently recased Nicholson north porch was to be moved to the west door, and the northern entrance eliminated, as marked on the 'plan as proposed'.

Inside the church the 14th century Neville Screen was to be removed to allow the presbytery to be extended into the eastern crossing of the Nine Altars, the new free-standing high altar being screened all round by canopied parclosing. The 17th century organ screen would be swept away to make room for a new screen in the more fashionable Gothic style of the period, and composed of elements derived from, if not physically salvaged from, the Neville Screen and Hatfield Monument. The whole screen was then to be surmounted by an elegant new Gothic organ case, for which the east and west elevations were given.

Externally the western towers were to receive the pinnacles and open parapets originally proposed by Wooler and Nicholson, but the central tower was to receive the most startling of Wyatt's proposed 'improvements'. The belfry stage of the tower was to be crowned by an upper octagonal stage supported by flying buttresses and surmounted by a short spire, very similar to one of Wyatt's designs for the tower at Fonthill Abbey on which he had started work in the same year, 1795.

Wyatt is said to have pronounced the chapter house ruinous, and in November 1795 the Dean and Chapter ordered it to be taken down, instructing Morpeth to build a 'chapter room' on the site. [14] Wyatt's original plan had shown the chapter house reduced in length but still with an apsidal east end, but this scheme was not followed by Morpeth, the often repeated story being that the latter demolished the chapter house vault by having the keystones knocked out, so allowing it to collapse onto the floor and ancient tomb-slabs below. During 1796 preparations were being made for demolishing the Galilee, but by the end of the year the Chapter had reversed its earlier decision and repaired the roof, largely because of pressure of public opinion, due in particular to the activities of John Carter in the Society of Antiquaries of London, on whose behalf he had begun to make measured record drawings of the cathedral in 1795.

The folio of drawings includes two designs for the east front of the Nine Altars Chapel. The first belongs to the original set as listed in Wyatt's fee account, and shows the facade almost exactly as reconstructed, with the 15th century tracery eliminated from all the lancet windows, but retaining the 15th century tracery forms of the rose window surrounded by sunk blank cusping. The upper parts of the great central buttresses were to be trimmed down, and the large canopied niches, which Hutchinson's plate had shown containing colossal figures, were to be eliminated.[15] The second drawing presents a much more fanciful design with elaborate pinnacles to the intermediate buttresses, and retaining the 15th century tracery in all the windows - much more the sort of design which might have appealed to 18th century clients (Figs. 38, 39).

The likely sequence of repair operations on the east front is that Nicholson had started paring down and re-dressing the buttresses, and may have begun to renew the external window dressings, nook-shafts and arches, including the Perpendicular tracery filling the lancets. Certainly the renewed jambs of the lower lancets do have later piecings-in at exactly the points where the tracery and transoms of the 15th-century-type windows would occur and which still survive (though renewed) in the south windows of the Nine Altars Chapel. Wyatt probably decided to restore the lancets to their original form, as shown in his first drawing of 1795, and this was the design which Morpeth eventually followed in completing the upper parts of the facade including replacing the old lead-covered spirelet of the south east turret with the present stone one. The tracery of the rose window was renewed, following the overall design of the 15th century tracery which had replaced the early tracery in the 13th century oculus, but not necessarily following the 15th century details. Wooler's recent north-east spire was left alone. A significant change in the reapirs was that Wyatt (or Morpeth) decided to reface the upper parts of the east front in new stone rather than dressing back the old surfaces, so setting the pattern for the refacings which were to proceed all along the south side of the cathedral during the next fifty years.

James Wyatt's total bill for his work for the Dean and Chapter came to £260 10s. 0d., made up of £150 for his time and expenses in carrying out his survey in 1795, £100 for providing the set of designs in 1975, and £10 10s. in 1797 for supplying detailed drawings for the work on the east front. As with the Wooler and Nicholson repairs, it is quite evident that Wyatt acted as the outside consultant or adviser, and that the executant architect was Morpeth.

There are several references to slating in the Chapter Minutes between 1798 and 1803, but these simple entries conceal completely the extent of Morpeth's work on the main roofs. He removed entirely the ancient oak high-pitched nave roof, shown in Carter's long section, and replaced it with the present lower pitched queen-post truss roof, with the ridge line brought down to match those of the quire and transepts. The old nave roof-line can still be distinguished on the west face of the central tower, and in the steep west gable of the nave between the western towers, where the gable apex now stands some ten feet above the new ridge. Morpeth's treatment of the quire roof was not quite so drastic - here he left the old late-mediaeval collared and strutted trusses and their purlins in position. The lead coverings of the nave, quire and Nine Altars roofs were replaced with Lakeland slates at this time. The sale of lead at this date would have virtually paid for the new slating, and the change of material seems to have been suggested by Wyatt.

The other work in progress on the cathedral at this time was the construction of the open parapets and 'ragged pinnacles' (that is, crocketted pinnacles) on the western towers, originally suggested by Wooler and revived in Wyatt's proposals. An engraving in *The Beauties of England and Wales*, published in 1801, indicates that the parapets were already in

Fig. 38 East front of Chapel of Nine Altars, 1777, drawn by George Nicholson

position on the north-west tower, the scaffolding being shown.[16] The old late mediaeval revestry on the south side of the quire was also demolished in 1801-1802 under Morpeth's direction, in what was to be a long continuing and ill-advised campaign to denude the cathedral of many of its surviving later mediaeval additions and insertions, all intended to restore the building to its original and pure 'Norman' state.

In 1803 attention was being turned towards the condition of the great tower, and in 1804 the Chapter sought the advice of another consultant William Atkinson (1773-1839).[17] He had been born at Bishop Auckland, where his father had been working as a builder on the castle. The young Atkinson attracted the attention of Wyatt, and he must have trained under Wyatt as well as at the Royal Academy Schools. His report to the Dean and Chapter dated 1804 is of the greatest interest in that it illustrates the changing attitudes to 'Restoration' and the reaction

Fig. 39 East front of Chapel of Nine Altars as proposed by James Wyatt, 1795

against the masonry re-dressing of Wooler and Nicholson.[18] He was anxious to retain the mossy and aged appearance of the tower, quoting from Burke on the 'Sublime', and to help achieve this, he proposed the use of Parker's Cement. Inside the cathedral he condemned the then current regular re-limewashing of the stonework, and made proposals for increasing the number of seats in the quire, which was a pressing need.

On Atkinson's recommendation, the well-known Italian plasterer Francesco Bernasconi was engaged, and work started on the south side of the tower in 1806, the Chapter stipulating that Atkinson and Bernasconi "include in their estimate the charge of producing the Effect of Roughness and the Appearance of Antiquity."[19] The work on plastering or cementing the tower proceeded through 1807, but by the summer of 1808 some members of the Chapter were dissatisfied with the results being achieved, and the work was suspended. On 20 July 1809 it was agreed to settle Mr Atkinson's and Mr Bernasconi's bills, and this brought to an end Atkinson's well-intentioned but less than fortunate connection with the cathedral. All the cement work had to be removed from the upper stages of the tower under the direction of Scott in the 1850s, but some of the Parker's Cement statues with brick cores still survive in the refectory undercroft, and the cement is indeed harder than many natural stones. The fronts of two of the prebendal houses, Nos.9 and 12 The College, were refaced at this time using the Parker's or Atkinson's Cement and illustrate the qualities and limitations of the material.

Purification, 1827 to 1858

The next main phase of restoration work was to start in 1827 with John Banks Jenkinson, Bishop of St David's, as dean from 1827-1840, and was to entail the refacing of practically the whole south front of the cathedral in new stone, in contrast to the dressing back of the north front masonry under the previous regimes. The work was commenced on the south front and gable of the Nine Altars and the south-west buttress and turret of the chapel, picking up at the point where Morpeth had rebuilt the upper part of the south-east turret in 1812-13. Thomas Jackson was the mason contractor for the work, and Ignatius Bonomi was to be the supervising or consultant architect. Bonomi (1787-1870) was a Durham-based architect who had an extensive practice in Northumberland, Durham and Yorkshire in the first half of the 19th century, confident in a variety of styles to suit the occasion. It was not surprising, therefore, that he made a careful restoration of the 15th century tracery to the four pairs of lancets in the south wall of the Nine Altars Chapel. He used the grouped lancets of the 13th century St Edmund's Chapel, Gateshead, as the model for reconstructing the gable itself.[20] His design for rebuilding the south-west turret and spire of the Chapel is more elaborate that the south-east turret by Wyatt or Morpeth, and he made a very positive effort to reproduce the original mouldings and caps, and the bird and beast enrichments, which are one of the delights of closely examining the surviving high-level sculpture of the Nine Altars interior.

Bonomi's restoration at the south end of the Nine Altars was carried out in new natural sandstone, as Wyatt's upper east front had been, this method being followed in all the further restoration work on the cathedral during the remainder of the 19th century. The stone used by Bonomi has weathered to a golden brown colour, and he used similar stone in his restorations of the south clerestory of the quire, and in the south gable and west face of the south transept between 1830 and 1835. He also provided the design for reconstructing the east wall of the slype, and took the first steps in opening up the interlacing arcading in the chapter house, which had been hidden behind the lath and plaster of Morpeth's 'Chapter Room'.

Anthony Salvin (1799-1881) succeeded Bonomi as consultant architect, and though of a Durham family in origin, he had been a pupil of John Nash, and his extensive practice remained London based. Much of 'his work for the university and cathedral in Durham was delegated to the Chapter's Clerk of Works. Salvin was engaged initially to design the new Grammar School, and the contracts for building the school were let in May 1843. In the same month he was urgently consulted about the structural failure of part of the crypt vault beneath the prebendal house which at that time was situated in the southern part of the dormitory, and his scheme for the essential repairs was put in hand speedily.

George Jackson, as Clerk of Works, had begun the restoration of the Decorated windows of the quire south aisle in March 1842, the work being carried out in a hard grey sandstone from

Fig. 40 Choir stalls and organ screen, 1680s to 1847

Fig. 41 Choir 1847-70, minus organ screen and with 17th century organ cut down and placed on north side

Gateshead Fell. By September 1842 Jackson had died, George Pickering being appointed Clerk of Works in his place, and he carried on the work by restoring the eastern aisle of the south transept, starting in February 1843. Here, for the first time, the latter mediaeval traceried windows were removed, and "replaced by the original Norman windows, traces of which were discovered."[21]

In the meantime, under the influence of George Waddington as dean (1840-1869), many changes were being made inside the cathedral as fundamental, and in many ways as disastrous for the interior of the cathedral, as those of the Reformation and the Civil War. The regular worship was still constricted within the quire by the great organ screen and the return stalls (Fig. 40); several attempts had been made to increase the number of sittings for the congregation in the choir stalls, and Pickering was preparing a further scheme in 1844. In 1846, according to the *Record*,

> "At the western end of the Choir, the wooden backs of the stalls on the North and South sides were removed, the tabernacle work, which ran in front of the pillars, was placed in the centre between them, following the line of the Hatfield monument; and thus the whole space between the pillars, North and South, was added to the width of the Choir. By this change twenty-two stalls were gained, and about thirty sittings."[22]

In 1844 the Tudor screen round the feretory "of in-different workmanship" was removed (renewed in the 1930's),[23] while in 1845 the marble font and its canopy were removed to the south-west corner of the nave so that the blocked west doorway could be opened up, to be filled by the present oak door, of Pickering's design.[24] What had survived of the 15th century oak screenwork round the Langley tomb was also taken down. The Castel clock case "of carved oak of inferior workmanship" was removed from the south transept (also to be restored in the 1930's).[25] Salvin designed a new stone pulpit for the quire in 1845, and new stone and marble altar rails in 1849. Mr Raine, the Chapter Librarian, had provided the design for a 'Norman' font in 1846, which was executed in Caen stone by Mr White of Pimlico. White also re-sorted the Neville Screen, and in 1849 was commissioned to execute in Caen stone an altar-piece of "Leonardo da Vinci's Last Supper" to be erected above the high altar.[26]

The year 1847 was momentous for the interior of the cathedral, for as the *Record* states,

> "The Organ Screen - a work of Charles II's time - in oak, boldly and not unskilfully carved, but after designs wholly inappropriate to a place of worship, was altogether removed, as were the stalls which were placed against it. The Nave and Transept were thus no longer severed from the Choir, but were immediately made available to the public for religious purpose. The Organ, under the superintendence of Mr Bishop, the organ builder, was placed on the North side of the Choir, under that arch immediately facing Bishop Hatfield's monument."[27]

Evidently the removal of the screen and resiting the organ on the north side of the quire pleased the Chapter, the scheme being confirmed and made permanent on 20th November 1847 (Fig. 41).

These extracts from the *Record* written by or at the instigation of Dean Waddington illustrate the mid-19th century attitude to how a great cathedral interior should be treated, banishing monuments and fittings which where not in the taste of the period. Salvin has been blamed for much that was done, but though his advice may have been sought unofficially, the quire pulpit and altar rails are the only items specifically linked with his name in the Chapter

Minutes at this time. (Both features have since been removed). Pickering certainly did a drawing for the new wooden west door, and he must have been involved in many of the other alterations.

During these years of internal re-arrangements to furnishings in the cathedral, work had been proceeding steadily on the fabric itself. In 1847 Salvin was renewing the window tracery of the large Decorated windows to the north quire aisle. Rather than restore the windows in their existing forms, which he must have considered debased, Salvin introduced three designs of his own, derived from windows in Sleaford and Holbeach churches in Lincolnshire and Boushton Aluph in Kent. Stained glass had been provided for the rose window in 1839, and for the north window of the Nine Altars in 1847. The same year saw the removal of the tracery from the windows to the north clerestory of the quire and they were restored to their original Normal forms; so were all the windows of the north triforium of the nave, and the large Geometric window at the end of the north transept was reglazed. Work continued with the windows of the north aisle of the Nave in 1848, the Perpendicular tracery being removed and the original Norman surrounds and nook-shafts restored, and plain glass inserted. The windows at the western extremeties of the north and south aisles were also deprived of their tracery and restored to their Norman forms.[28]

George Pickering reported directly to the Chapter in 1849 on the serious state of the external masonry to the south aisle of the nave. The total refacing of the aisle in new stone followed, under his direction, the proposals being subject to the approval of Salvin. All the later Gothic traceried windows were changed back to Norman, and the evidence of the earlier gablets to the aisle triforium was obliterated, though Salvin did produce a scheme for restoring the aisle gables. The nave south and north clerestories were also refaced, and their windows lost their tracery, all this Pickering work being in a grey stone. In due course this cycle of window 'restoration' was completed with the east aisle of the north transept, only the west face of this transept escaping, and preserving something of the charm of later mediaeval tracery within Romanesque window surrounds. The cathedral is indeed fortunate that much of the original mediaeval window tracery has survived in the great 'terminal' windows, at the west end and in the transepts. There never seems to have been any intention of restoring the conjectural Romanesque windows to the end gables of the nave and transepts.

Scholarly Repairs, 1858 to 1933

The next major work on the cathedral was to be the restoration of the belfry stage of the central tower, for ever since Atkinson's cement-work repairs to the belfry had been summarily suspended by the Chapter in 1808, the appearance of the tower must have been of concern. The Great Chapter of 20 November 1858 agreed that the upper parapet be restored in stone "according to plans to be approved by Mr Gilbert Scott of London .... the celebrated mediaeval Architect."[29] He was asked also to submit plans and specifications for the eventual restoration of the belfry and removal of the cement.

The future Sir George Gilbert Scott (1811-1878) was the most successful Gothic Revival architect of his generation; by the end of his career he had carried out restoration or furnishing work on at least twenty English and Welsh cathedrals. Between November 1858 and January 1859 he produced proposals for restoring the Durham belfry at an estimated cost of £5,500; this was approved by the Chapter on 21 January 1859, and the work was completed in 1860,

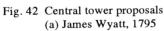

Fig. 42 Central tower proposals
(a) James Wyatt, 1795

(b) Sir George Gilbert Scott, 1860

the entire belfry being refaced in Prudham and Dunhouse stone. A Special Chapter was held on 6 March 1860 "to consider Mr Scott's designs for the termination of the Central Tower, when it was agreed that the work be completed so as to restore to the Tower the same Architectural features which it possessed when the Cement was placed upon it."[30] Just as his predecessors Wooler, Nicholson and Wyatt had felt the need to 'improve' the top of the central tower, so did Gilbert Scott, and his proposals were even more startling than those of Wyatt (Fig. 42a, b). His intention was to construct an open crown on flying buttresses supported by great pinnacles, similar to but on a larger scale than the 15th century corona of St Nicholas, Newcastle, which Scott was to restore so expertly. However, the Chapter restricted Scott to heightening the pierced battlements and the little square pinnacles surmounting the corner buttresses. This preserved the unique tapering silhouette of the Durham tower which is given by the canopied offsets of its slender corner buttresses. A note in the library suggests that it was Robson, the Chapter's Clerk of Works and deputy to Scott, who advised the Chapter to reject Scott's scheme, mainly on structural grounds, and in this he was almost certainly right.

Edward Robert Robson (1836-1917), a Durham man and son of a local builder who had trained with Dobson in Newcastle and Scott in London, proceeded with repairs to the west face and north-west corner of the Galilee Chapel in 1863 and may have been responsible for the careful restoration of the north door to the chapel. On his resignation in 1864, he was succeeded as Clerk of Works by Charles Hodgson Fowler, then aged twenty four, another of Scott's protegés. Hodgson Fowler (1840-1910) continued the work on the Galilee Chapel and prepared schemes for additions to the Grammar School and various works on College houses. He reported on fractures in a pinnacle and several pilasters of the western towers in July 1866, but though estimates for the repairs were obtained, the Chapter made no immediate decision on them. However, restoration of the exterior of the College gate was commenced in August 1867. Dean Waddington offered to fill the great western window with stained glass in April 1867 and the south transept window also was filled with stained glass at this time, retaining the surviving mediaeval painted glass in some of the tracery lights. Clayton and Bell made the new glazing to both of these windows.

Sir Gilbert Scott was recalled to Durham in 1870 and by 1876 the triple-arched marble quire screen was built and the Cosmati work marble pulpit provided, together with the letten brass Pelican lectern.[31] But the most important contributions at this time were Scott's superb marble pavement to the quire and sanctuary in Opus Alexandrium, and the restoration of the choir stalls and tabernacle canopies to something very like their 17th century arrangements, after having been cut up and set back between the piers in the 1840s. Scott was now towards the end of his career, and at least where the stalls are concerned, some of the credit for their restoration must be attributable to his pupil, Hodgson Fowler, who would have been in charge of the work.

Much criticism has been levelled at Scott's quire screen during those years when High Victorian design was out of favour. Yet in the thirty years between the removal of the organ screen and the erection of the new screen, the 'grand vista' from west to east in the cathedral had come to be considered somewhat disappointing and lacking in visual punctuation. The Scott screen is simple and bold in concept, and whatever one thinks of its detailed design, it does provide the necessary element that had been missing and which gives incident and scale to the whole interior of the building.

During the middle years of the 19th century a series of ecclesiastical reforms were affecting all cathedral chapters, and one of the results was that the Architect to the Ecclesiastical Commissioners, Ewan Christian, visited Durham in 1870 to assess the state of the cathedral fabric and the cost of repairs required within the next twenty years. Christian's report to the Commission was dated 1 December 1870 and was quite short. He deplored the "Wyatt" repairs (everyone continued to blame Wyatt for the Wooler and Nicholson re-dressing until the 1950s), and rightly pointed out that the cutting away of the stone surfaces would lead to much more difficult repair problems in the future. He was concerned about the state of the internal flying buttresses to the triforia, but gave first priority to repairs needed to the open arcading in the upper parts of the western towers. These he considered would cost £14,000, and should be undertaken immediately. He commented on the poor state of some of the lead-covered roofs, and inside the cathedral he commented, as Atkinson had done in 1804, on the need to remove the encrustations of whitewash from the stonework, and noted this had been done successfully at that time in the north aisle.[32]

Most of the works on which Christian reported were to be carried out in the following years. The remainder of the internal stonework was cleaned of the whitewash or limewash in all but the least visible parts of the building, and the upper arcading of the western towers was extensively renewed. This work on the towers will have been undertaken by Hodgson Fowler, and it was he who designed the twin organ cases in the quire surmounting the stall canopies. Hodgson Fowler was made Architect to the Dean and Chapter of Durham in 1885, and he is best remembered for his reconstruction of the chapter house as a memorial to Bishop Lightfoot in 1892. Some work had been commenced on restoring the chapter house in 1847 when the western entrance, sealed up by Morpeth, was re-opened, and some of the arcading which had been hidden by lath and plaster was revealed. In 1857 the great west window to the chapter room was re-opened, and the west wall of the chapter house restored, in association with repair work on the cloister. Hodgson Fowler had a fair amount of evidence on which to base his design for rebuilding the eastern apse of the chapter house, in the form of engravings. But for some reason he did not quite follow the plan of the apse ribs, for his keystone at the junction of the apse ribs differs in certain details from the original keystone, which still survives. Of interest in structural terms is his use of concrete for the vault cells rather than rubble masonry - one of his few concessions to more modern constructional methods, even if he did use the material in much the way that Roman engineers would have done.

Hodgson Fowler was succeeded as Consultant Architect by Mervyn Edmund Macartney (1853-1932), later Sir Mervyn, who is best known for his Surveyorship of St. Paul's Cathedral. At Durham he was asked to inspect the cathedral buildings twice each year, and two of his brief reports survive from 1913 and 1914. In the first of these he was commenting upon another report by W.D. Caröe, and the second was issued jointly with Mr Caröe. William Douglas Caröe (1857-1938) had trained with John L. Pearson, had become Architect to the Ecclesiastical Commissioners in succession to Ewan Christian, and in due course advised on the repairs of many cathedrals and churches. He had surveyed parts of Durham Cathedral previously for the Commissioners, and made a further detailed examination of the structure on 31 July and 1 August 1913. He was mainly concerned about the condition of the distorted semi-circular arches over the quire triforia, and the quadrant flying buttresses of the nave triforium, as well as various matters in the Galilee Chapel and central tower.

In 1915 major repairs were begun on the nave vault, following the reports by Macartney and Caröe. Under the direction of Macartney, two extra rings of stone were inserted under the nave triforium quadrant arches, making them into very solid internal flying buttresses to abut the thrust from the nave vault, while steel tie rods were placed above the high vault to restrain any outward movement in the clerestory walls. This work caused an absolute storm within the Society of Antiquaries of London, and the Society commissioned three fellows to report.[33] They agreed that the work was unnecessary and was destroying the historical integrity of the structure. We have no record of Macartney's views, but at least the rent in the nave vault originally reported by Wooler in 1777 was solidly repaired, and no movement has shown itself in the nave structure since. On the other hand, Caröe had thought the quire triforium transverse arches worse than the nave, and yet virtually nothing has been done to them since 1913, and they seem none the worse for it.

In his 1913 report Caröe had expressed concern about the central tower and its lantern vault, partly because of the design of the structure, and partly from the effects of bell ringing. He amplified his concern in a further report dated July 1922, and was commissioned by the Chapter to undertake the necessary structural repairs that year. Displaced vault-rib stones were eased back into place, cracks in the ringing chamber walls were cement-grouted and stitched with tiles, while the whole bell frame and its supporting structure was tightened up and braced as far as possible. The project inside the cathedral for which Caröe was responsible at this time was the design of the Durham Light Infantry memorial Chapel and its elaborate oak screening. The marble monument listing all the bishops, priors and deans of Durham was designed in 1929 by Wood and Oakley, who were the successors of C.H. Fowler's practice, and they also modified the oak parclose screens either side of the sanctuary. Outside, the parapets and pinnacles of the two western towers were reconstructed between 1930 and 1933 under the direction of Reginald Annandale Cordingley (1896-1962), then head of the School of Architecture in Newcastle. It was at this period that there had been considerable concern over the stability of the Galilee Chapel, at a time when extensive engineering works were found necessary to prevent the castle slipping towards the river.

Care and Conservation, 1933 to 1993

The advent of Dean Cyril Alington in 1933 may be taken as the beginning of the modern period, characterised by efforts to rectify what in our conservation-conscious era we deem the ravages of the past. Thus, the remaining fragments of the 17th century screen and organ were assembled near the west end of the south aisle under Cordingley's direction, while the feretory screen was renewed, copying sections which had survived. The elegant 17th century marble font was brought out of retirement at Pittington, and perhaps most important, the Castel Clock was reinstated in the south transept. Dean Alington listened to the advice of Stephen Dykes Bower for much of this work, and it was he who designed the silver cross and candlesticks for the Bede Altar in the Chapel of the Nine Altars in 1935. As successors to Cordingly, Donald McIntyre and Matthew Hayton had designed the oak 'birdcage' lectern in 1939, which supplanted Scott's brass pelican until 1990, and was intended to have a tall 'Cosin Gothic' canopy.

After the Second War, with John Wild as dean, it was Sir Ninian Comper (1864-1960) who was to design the hanging tester over the feretory, with Donald McIntrye (until 1969) and Matthew Hayton (until 1973) continuing as resident architects to the cathedral, and with George Gaze Pace (1915-1975) as Consultant Architect from 1955 until his death. Ian Curry succeeded him in 1976. Major repairs to the stonework of the north transept had been undertaken in 1951, and to the Priory Kitchen in 1969, while the north-west spirelet of the Nine Altars Chapel was rebuilt in 1962. New underfloor heating was installed between 1967 and 1969. Pace designed the new gold and ebony reredos in the Gregory Chapel in 1959 (modified and resited 1989), restored the 17th century choir pulpit in 1964, and designed the Galilee cross and Bede memorial in 1967 and 1970 respectively. His were the designs for reglazing the north aisle of the nave, the Galilee Chapel and refectory, between 1965 and 1970, the new entrance to the Deanery in 1974 and the display bookcases in the spendement in 1973. His office adapted part of the dormitory undercroft as bookshop and restaurant in 1975. It was Ian Curry who in 1978 designed the new treasury in the middle part of the undercroft, the casing to the choir organ, the reconstruction of the choir music library on the site of the revestry in 1985, and the new oak lobbies to the north and south doors in the cathedral.

The repair works of the past twenty years have concentrated on roof coverings and stonework; re-slating of the quire and Nine Altars roofs (1972-1977), during which the 1830 refaced masonry of the south quire clerestory had be be re-secured to the core walling; and reslating the nave and north transept roofs (1987-1990), all in Lakeland slate, together with renewal of associated leadwork.

In 1982 a long-term programme of masonry repairs was begun which will have to include all the stonework that was re-dressed or cut back at the end of the 18th century, that is, the western towers, north front and east end. Starting at the southern end of the Chapel of the Nine Altars, extensive repairs have been made to the masonry of the east front including stabilising its centre gable (1982-1992); it will then go on to the north-east spirelet of the chapel. Continuing from the work on the quire roof, the plasterwork of the quire vaults were repaired, cleaned, and redecorated (1990-1991). In the central tower the bells were re-hung in a new frame in 1980, the 1922 stiffening of the old framework having proved ineffective, while in 1990-1991 the intermediate pinnacles of the central tower were being extensively repaired, the stones used in the 1865 repairs having eroded to an alarming extent.

Our survey is completed, then, but the story has no ending, for the work continues. Indeed, projects appear to multiply. A mere forty years of Anglo-Norman building thus set in motion centuries of Romanesque aftercare. It has been, and is, literally, a never-ending challenge.

Acknowledgement

This Chapter is based on the Durham Lecture, 1985, given by the author, entitled 'Sense and Sensitivity - Durham Cathedral and its Architects', and published by the Dean and Chapter of Durham in 1985.

Plate I. Nave south aisle: dado arcade and 13th-century decorative painting, including chevrons on the respond.

Plate II. Refectory, east wall: detail of 12th-century paintings, showing a king and other figures. (Crown Copyright).

Plate IV. Prior's Chapel (now Deanery): Adoration of the Child,
c.1475-80. (Crown Copyright)

Plate III. Galilee Chapel, northern altar recess: St. Cuthbert,
c.1180. (Crown Copyright).

4 The Interior Decoration of the Cathedral

David Park

> '...wch cover was all gilded over and of eyther side was painted fower lively Images curious to ye beholders and on the East End was painted the picture of or Savio^r sittinge on a Rainebowe to geive Judgm^t very lively to ye beholders and on the West end of itt was the picture of o^r Lady & o^r Savio^r on her knee....'

The above description of the cover over St Cuthbert's shrine is only one of hundreds of references to paintings, carvings and other decoration in the *Rites of Durham*.[1] Although dating from the 1590s, the *Rites* describes the cathedral and monastery as they were just before the Reformation. Almost certainly by a former monk of Durham, it provides a unique record of how a cathedral looked and functioned in the late Middle Ages: not as the relatively empty building we see today but crowded with altars and other furnishings; not as an isolated church but as an integral part of one of the greatest monasteries in Europe. Therefore, in this chapter although the focus will be on surviving painted decoration in the cathedral, it will also include the equally interesting but little known paintings in the monastic buildings, and try to set all these - albeit superficially - within the context of the many other furnishings that contributed to the 'decoration' of both cathedral and monastery.

One all-pervading theme in the decoration was St Cuthbert himself, whose shrine was the major focus of pilgrimage in northern England. In the late Middle Ages, as we know from the *Rites* and other sources, he was depicted in more than eighteen windows in the cloister and elsewhere; much of this glass was given by Bishop Langley (1406-37), and must have resembled the surviving St Cuthbert window also given by him to York Minster. But only a few images of the saint now survive at Durham, most notably the celebrated late 12th-century wall painting in the Galilee Chapel (Pl.III), where he is accompanied by St Oswald (the Northumbrian royal martyr whose head was kept in Cuthbert's shrine). Of similar date is a highly important but virtually unknown wall painting concealed by panelling in what was originally the monks' refectory, and is now the Chapter Library. Discovered in 1962, this painting on the east wall has been severely keyed for a later layer of plaster, but at the south end a number of large standing figures can still be made out including a bishop and a king (Pl.II), while at the other end a 'recumbent figure of a man, with head thrown back and arms raised' is recorded. Since it was a well-established tradition to represent a monastery's patron or patron saint in the refectory, these paintings must almost certainly show St Cuthbert.[2] They would have formed a fitting backdrop to the great feast of St Cuthbert held every year on the day of his death.

Although the *Rites* affords a marvellous impression of the appearance of the cathedral in the later Middle Ages, it is less useful for understanding the early decoration of a building whose impact now results chiefly from its enormously powerful Romanesque architecture. Much the most striking decorative effect in the Romanesque building is created by the lozenges, chevrons and spirals carved deeply into the piers. Carved decoration of this type - at least on such an enormous scale - seems to be a Durham innovation, and subsequently reappears in other buildings dependent on or influenced by it, as mentioned in chapter 2. The spirally grooved piers, consistently associated with important features such as altars, appear to be 'meaningful' in that sense, and depend on a tradition extending back to the Early Christain period.[3] Although this architectural carving may originally have been coloured, there is now apparently no trace of *any* painting in the cathedral to be associated with the original building. Doubtless some existed, including perhaps figure-subjects in important locations, but in general it seems that the decoration of early Romanesque buildings was often as austere as their architecture - at Winchester Cathedral, for example, examination of the 11th-century transepts has revealed that the main or perhaps only decorative effect was achieved by the prominent white pointing of the masonry itself.[4] There are, however, surviving continental examples of Romanesque buildings with elaborately painted piers, and very likely the carved decoration at Durham represents a more expensive version of similar painted decoration once existing in England. At Exeter, late 11th-century columns from St Nicholas' Priory were found to be painted with spirals, and lozenge and scale patterns; and a fragment of painting of similar date from St Mary's Abbey, York, also has a lozenge design very like that occurring in Durham.

In the late Romanesque and early Gothic additions to the cathedral, a polychromatic effect was achieved partly by the very effective contrast of the buff-coloured sandstone masonry with limestone polished to resemble marble. The Galilee Chapel at the west end, dating from c.1175-80, shows an exceptionally early use of Purbeck marble in the shafts (paired with freestone shafts) in the arcades, while the Nine Altars Chapel at the east end, begun in the 1240s, has a splendid array of shafts in the local Frosterley marble, in which a curious 'splodgy' effect is created by the large coral fossils. This chapel also retains some of the earliest surviving architectural polychromy in the cathedral with remains of red, blue and black on the arcade enclosing the altars, and of further colouring in a few of the quatrefoils above. Also from the mid 13th century are simple, but exquisitely executed, painted decorative motifs, reflecting the same restrained taste as the grisaille glass used contemporaneously in the cathedral's windows.[5] In the prior's chapel (now part of the Deanery), dating from between 1244 and 1254, the foliate decoration on a jamb of one of the lancet windows (Fig.43) shows, in its squared forms, the taste for ornament based on Cufic lettering characteristic of 13th-century painting elsewhere (for example, on draperies in the Westminster Retable). The vigorous painted scrollwork on the north doorway of the chapel, black on the jamb and a striking turquoise-blue on the soffit, is typically mid 13th century in its stylised forms, as in the prominent 'trefoil-ended stalks'.

The survival of similar decoration in the cathedral itself indicates that in the 13th century the Romanesque building - as at Ely, Peterborough, and elsewhere - was given at least a partial 'face-lift' through painted ornament. In the south transept there are remains of foliate scrollwork with flowers and a trefoil-ended stalk on the wall of the northernmost altar, and similar ornament survives on an adjacent Romanesque capital. But the most extensive survival of the 13th-century decoration overlaying the original Romanesque architecture is in the blind arcading in one bay of the nave south aisle: here one section has been reproduced in modern repainting, clearly showing the scheme of masonry pattern (lining imitating the joints between blocks of masonry), scrollwork and stencilled rosettes, while traces of delicate foliate sprays survive in some of the spandrels above (see Pl.I). Fragments of this scheme also survive in the vaulting of the aisle - foliate decoration on a rib and arch soffit - and probably also of the same date is the design of repeated four-petalled motifs (somewhat reminiscent in appearance of carved dogtooth) discovered in 1990 on the soffit of the south-east doorway. Most

Fig. 43 Prior's Chapel (now Deanery): 13th-century foliate ornament on window jamb, based on Cufic lettering

Fig. 44 Galilee Chapel: damaged scene of the Coronation of the Virgin above the northern altar recess, with figure of St. Cuthbert blessing to the right (c.1300)

interestingly, the bold black chevrons painted on one of the aisle responds deliberately imitate - over a century later - the carved chevrons of the pier opposite. Nor was this type of imitation confined to Durham itself; at nearby Finchale Priory, the 13th-century choir piers were painted with chevrons and other geometric designs in a clear reference to the mother house - in what indeed could be termed the Durham 'house style'.[6]

While at least some of the architectural polychromy of the cathedral can be pieced together from surviving fragments, another type of painted decoration - of the many stone and wooden screens dividing the internal spaces of the cathedral - is more difficult to reconstruct. The *Rites* describes a screen across the east end of the nave, with 'the whole stories & passion of our Lord wroughte in stone most curiously & most fynely gilte, & also above... was all the storie and pictures of the XII apostles... very fynelie gilte'. Two panels from this screen, datable to c.1155, still survive, one showing the Transfiguration and the other Christ appearing to Mary Magdalene and to the two Marys after the Resurrection, but nothing remains of 'the most goodly & famous Roode [crucifix]' that was set above the screen. In general, pitifully little is known about roods and their screens at this period, but some light on the Durham arrangement may be shed by paintings elsewhere that were originally associated with roods. At Kempley (Glos.), the nave east wall paintings of c.1130 undoubtedly once framed a sculptured rood, and include a representation of the Marys at the Sepulchre (symbolising the Resurrection) on the south side. At Ickleton (Cambs.), approximately contemporary paintings on the nave north wall comprise, like the Durham screen, scenes of the apostles (all martyrdom subjects) and of

Plate V. Durham Cathedral, nave interior looking north-east.

Plate VI. Durham Cathedral looking east along the south aisle, watercolour by J.M.W. Turner, 1797-8.

Christ's Passion, and end with the Carrying of the Cross; the Crucifixion itself was probably represented in the form of a carved rood at the crossing, followed by post-Crucifixion scenes painted on the south wall.[7] It seems very likely, therefore, that the iconography of the Durham screen was by no means untypical, that the apostle scenes were mostly martyrdom subjects, and that the Christological series began with Passion scenes to the north of and 'preceding' the crucifix, and ended with post-Resurrection scenes 'following' it to the south. Various other screens in the cathedral are described in the *Rites*, such as the choir screen with carved images of kings and bishops, and such smaller examples as the painted wooden screens dividing the altars in the Nine Altars Chapel. Here, there were doubtless screens between the altars originally, but from the description of the painting as 'branches & flowers and other imagerye most finely... pictured and guilted', it would seem that this decoration, at least, was of later medieval date.

It was, of course, partly to provide more altars at which the monks could celebrate that the Nine Altars Chapel was constructed. In addition to the normal daily round of worship, some of the most important liturgical ceremonies of the year were associated with Easter. From Easter to Ascension, a huge bronze paschal candlestick was erected before the high altar; almost certainly of 12th-century date, and so enormous that it could only be lit through a hole in the vault, its decoration included flying dragons, flowers, crystals and armed horsemen as well as the evangelists. Normally kept disassembled in the north choir aisle, it was polished each year by children from the almshouses before being erected.[8] Another object with a specific use at Easter was a curious image of the Virgin, Our Lady of Bolton, to whom an altar in the south transept was dedicated. This sculpture is described in the *Rites* as

'a m^{r}veylous lyvelye and bewtifull Image of the picture of our Ladie... whiche picture was maide to open wth gym[mers] [or two leaves] from her breaste downdward. And wth in ^{ye} said image was wrowghte and pictured the Image of our saviour, m[ar]veylouse fynlie gilted houlydinge vppe his handes, and holding betwixt his handes a fair & large crucifix of christ, all of gold'.

At Easter, this crucifix was taken out and displayed in the choir, and then every monk 'did crepe uvto it that was in ye churche as the Daye', before its symbolic burial in a temporary sepulchre. It must have been a rare example in England of a *Schreinmaddona*, a type first introduced c.1300 and of which examples still exist in Germany.[9]

Our Lady of Bolton was just one of scores of images of the Virgin in the medieval cathedral. For instance, she occupied the central position of the Neville Screen, erected in 1376-9 largely at the cost of John Lord Neville. This screen, still a mangificant backdrop to the high altar, was prefabricated in London and sent up in boxes via Newcastle; originally its central images were alabaster figures of the Virgin flanked by SS. Cuthbert and Oswald, 'all richly gilded'.[10] That this late medieval composition may well have reflected an earlier arrangement at the east end is suggested by the late 12th-century paintings in the Galilee Chapel. Here, the jambs of the northern altar recess are painted with life-size figures of St Cuthbert (Pl.III) and St Oswald, and the back wall with imitation draperies but with a vertical strip in the centre left plain probably to accommodate a carved image. Evidence that this altar was dedicated to the Virgin is provided by two references: a charter of the 1180s, referring to an altar of St Mary in the Galilee (though without stating its position); and the *Rites* reference to an altar of Our Lady on the north side of the chapel. Originally, therefore, it may well have contained a central sculptured image of the Virgin, while additional confirmation of the

Fig. 45 Galilee Chapel: Crucifixion (with Adam below rising from his grave and holding a chalice), flanked by the martyrdoms of SS. Peter and Paul (c. 1300)

Fig. 46 Galilee Chapel: Martyrdom of St. Paul (c. 1300)

Fig. 47 Tomb of Bishop Thomas Hatfield (d. 1381): angel at the foot of the bishop's effigy

Fig. 48 Prior's Chapel now Deanery: detail of the Resurrection (c. 1475-80)

dedication is provided by a painting of c.1300 on the wall directly above. Although only the lower half survives, the painting clearly showed the Coronation of the Virgin within a circular frame, once again with a figure of St Cuthbert to the right (Fig.44).[11] This altar of the Virgin would have been particularly suited to the devotions of women, who were not allowed access to the main body of the church, and such a use is perfectly captured in the 1180s charter, in its reference to a husband and son offering a gift to St Cuthbert's altar in the church, but the wife to Mary's altar in the Galilee.

On the south wall of this aisle in the Galilee is the only extensive series of painted figure-subjects in the cathedral. They belong to the same scheme as the Coronation of the Virgin on the east wall, and the combination of subjects is reminiscent of the 12th-century rood screen: a central Crucifixion flanked by scenes of the twelve apostles (the three westernmost are now lost), all set within a painted arcade of trefoil-headed arches. The Crucifixion, alone of the series, extends into the spandrel of the arcade below; here Adam is depicted rising from his grave and holding Christ's blood in a chalice, symbolising man's redemption through God's grace (Fig.45). The representations of the apostles include one of Doubting Thomas, oddly showing the saint with a rich fur lining to his cloak, but most are wonderfully vigorous martyrdom scenes. St. John is boiled in oil, St. Peter crucified upside down, and St. Paul beheaded - the executioner here grasping the long hair at the back of the saint's otherwise bald head (Fig. 46)! The black flesh of figures such as the executioner wielding an enormous ladle in the St. John scene is a particularly striking feature. It might be thought to signify evil were it not that Adam and the Virgin, for example, show the same characteristic. In fact, these black areas were scientifically examined in 1991, and found to be lead white pigment that had subsequently altered; this is a widespread phenomenon in medieval wall paintings, occurring most famously in those by Cimabue in the upper church at Assisi.[12] No doubt the same explanation applied to the 12th-century refectory paintings, which, when found in the 1960s, were thought to be unfinished because of their black faces.

The 14th and 15th centuries saw, as in other great churches, a veritable invasion of the cathedral by magnificent tombs and chantry chapels. All lavishly decorated, and typically including elaborate displays of heraldry - reflecting the increased secularity of the age -, these monuments profoundly affected the interior appearance of the cathedral. A particularly important chantry was that of the Neville family in the south aisle of the nave, from which the splendid if battered tomb of John Lord Neville (d.1388) and his wife still survives. But the finest monuments at Durham were to the bishops themselves, previously more modestly interred in the chapter house. Among the first to receive such a memorial was Bishop Louis de Beaumont (d.1333). His enormous brass, stretching across the floor in front of the high altar and characteristically including figures of his ancestors 'in theire coate armour', was the largest and finest of its date in England, though only the indent now survives.[13] Even more ostentatious was the chantry of Bishop Thomas Langley (d.1437) located in the Galilee, and completely blocking the west doorway of the nave. The most prominent tomb of all, however, was that of Bishop Thomas Hatfield (d.1381) which still survives on the south side of the choir. In this amazing structure, built during Hatfield's lifetime, the tomb is combined with a throne above; the modern repainting and gilding, though distressingly gaudy, nevertheless afford some impression of the splendour of the original polychromy. Fine, though fragmentary, paintings still remain on the interior walls of the tomb: angels as heraldic supporters at the feet of the alabaster effigy (Fig.47), and, at its head angels taking Hatfield's

Plate VIII. Durham, watercolour by Felix Mendelssohn Bartholdy, 1829

Plate VII. Durham Cathedral, watercolour by J.S. Cotman, 1806

Plate X. God's factory at night, gouache by Robert Soden, 1982

Plate IX. Cathedral, oil on canvas, by Maureen Enright, 1982

soul to heaven in a napkin. Above the latter painting was a depiction of the Majesty displaying his wounds, now mostly lost but known from an 18th-century drawing.

The priors too indulged in lavish patronage in the late Middle Ages, providing, for instance, almost all the major stained glass of this period in the cathedral. Indeed, much the finest late medieval wall paintings still existing in the north of England were executed for one of their number, probably Richard Bell (1464-78) or Robert Ebchester (1478-84). Absurdly little-known, these paintings decorate the north wall of the prior's chapel (now the entrance hall to the Deanery) and were discovered behind panelling only in 1974. Four scenes are set within a painted architectural arcade, each illustrating a verse from a contemporary hymn to the Virgin contained in the border below. The first scene, the Annunciation, is badly damaged, but the seated figure of the Virgin with a lectern behind her can still be made out. Next is the Nativity (Pl. IV), in the late medieval form of the Adoration of the Child, deriving from the revelations of the 14th-century visionary, St Bridget of Sweden. The Christ Child is shown on the ground, lying on a cushion and surrounded by a glory, while the Virgin, Joseph and the midwife kneel in adoration. The Resurrection then follows, the Virgin kneeling on a tasselled cushion and worshipping Christ as he steps from the tomb, with two guards in elaborate plate armour to the left (Fig.48). Although little is visible of the fourth scene, enough remains of the inscription to identify it as the Ascension, and probably there was a final scene of the Virgin's own Assumption. Although major alterations to the prior's quarters are documented under John Wessington (1416-46), the style of the paintings and the evidence of the armour and costume - particularly the fashionable dress of the midwife, with her tight-fitting bodice, flat collar and loosely slung girdle - suggest a somewhat later date of c.1475-80. The only really comparable wall paintings from this period in England are the famous series in Eton College Chapel showing miracles of the Virgin, and likewise heavily influenced in style and iconography by contemporary Netherlandish painting. Whereas the Eton scenes are much more complex compositionally and show an interest in spatial setting almost entirely absent at Durham, their essentially grisaille palette is very subdued in contrast to the gorgeously coloured Durham paintings. Although the sophisticated technique at Durham has yet to be fully analysed, the blue pigment, for instance, has been identified as the vegetable dye indigo, applied in no fewer than three different ways.[14] No more fitting climax to the medieval decoration at Durham could be found than these superb paintings, venerating the Virgin like so many works before them.

5 An Architectural Appreciation

Sherban Cantacuzino

Like Ruskin I number the view from the railway station among the seven wonders of the world. Nowhere, except perhaps in Venice, is the sense of arrival greater. In crossing the lagoon from the mainland, expectations last longer, and the interior life of a metropolitan railway station has to be experienced before emerging in the bright sunlight of the Grand Canal. At Durham the train passes swiftly from cutting to viaduct before touching earth again on the hill that is the station, for it needed the courage of the Victorian railway engineer to enter the city at high level. Getting off the train and out of the modest station is quickly done, there on the forecourt below to relish the full splendour of a view already glimpsed in that fleeting moment on the viaduct. The myriad roofs of the city spread into the valley below and wrap around the acropolis that holds atop cathedral and castle. Rising from the roofs the sturdy tower of St Godric in Castle Chare and the elegant church spire of St Nicholas's in the Market Place are landmarks which lead the eye away and then back again to the visual climax on the rocky peninsula opposite. Yet the view is not exclusively, not even predominantly, brick, stone and slate. The green of the distant hills penetrates the city from all sides to gather in the luxuriance of the wooded hillside beneath the cathedral. This urban "lung" is important visually, not only because it relates to the countryside beyond, but also because it provides a substantial light-absorbent area, and therefore a contrast to the light-reflecting surfaces of surrounding buildings. On a fine day the soft dark mass of the wooded hillside contrasts sharply with the hard west faces of the castle and cathedral towers and transepts ablaze with sunlight.

If it was my love of Romanesque architecture which originally took me to Durham, this first view of the cathedral could not have been very reassuring with its Perpendicular crossing tower, Early English west towers and Decorated window tracery in the gable ends. The earlier Romanesque towers would no doubt have been shorter and would have terminated in pyramid roofs. The composition and massing seen from this view point would have been less satisfying. We must indeed be thankful to the master-mason, John Bell, for perceiving the inadequacy of his predecessor's work and raising the crossing tower by a further stage.

Rare if not quite unique is the combination of cathedral and castle in one composition. In the view from the station the castle hugs the hill, while the cathedral dominates it. Or, to adapt Frank Lloyd Wright's maxim, the castle is of the hill, whereas the cathedral stands on top of it. That here temporal power should have submitted to the superiority of spiritual power so unequivocally and with such grace is due perhaps to the fact that in the Middle Ages Durham was a County Palatine, with bishops wielding temporal as well as spiritual power in the manner of the prince-bishops of Germany.

To clamber from the station down to the roundabout and cross the River Wear is to enter the polluted and hostile world of the motor car. However daring the structure underneath, on it the modern Milburngate Bridge does not feel like a bridge leaping over a river but like the road for fast and heavy traffic that it is. An unavoidable and dismal interlude this may be, but it is greatly relieved by the view of Framwellgate Bridge, with the castle and cathedral somewhat fore-shortened now by the sheer slope of the hill, but still soaring above the trees.

Since I am trying to paint pictures, it is better to be looking at the two elliptical arches of the bridge from a certain distance than to be on top of them. Mercifully, having crossed the river, it is possible to take a slip road up and over the horrible 'motorway' into the Market Place, a contained space where all seems peace and quiet and from where the ascent of the acropolis may begin.

The way to the top is surprisingly short. Walking up Owengate, first the west towers of the cathedral, then the west end of the nave come into view before the narrow street gives way to the vast level space of Palace Green, the south side of which is taken up by the entire length of the cathedral. This is the same north face which we so greatly admired from the station when we saw it in perspective and in contrast to the sunlit faces of the towers and transepts. But here we are seeing the north face head on so that the full length of the cathedral appears to be more or less permanently in shadow, unrelieved by the building's sunlit faces which cannot be seen from this angle. Add to this the fact that the modelling of the exterior is rather flat and that there is effectively no west front because of the Galilee Chapel, and it becomes possible to understand why the exterior of the cathedral has sometimes been considered not quite worthy of the interior.

Construction began at the chancel end and, if we want to see what this early work was like, we must look at the east elevation of the transepts where the sequence from the bottom upwards in each bay is pairs of blind arches, large single round-headed windows with nook shafts and, for the gallery, pairs of tiny windows set in an arched panel. In the chancel aisles the large single windows were replaced in the 14th century by even larger windows with tracery of such invention that no two windows are alike. These windows look frivolous next to the austere Romanesque forms and are too large, so that the predominance of solid wall over window openings, a hall-mark of Romanesque architecture, begins to the challenged.

Transepts, crossing and chancel, which originally ended in three apses, were built by Bishop William of St Calais who also established a community of Benedictine monks and built the monastery. His successor, Bishop Flambard, built the nave, though the vault was only completed in 1133, five years after his death. The nave elevations are a continuation of the earlier work except at gallery level, where the tiny twin windows are replaced by a single round-headed opening, making this part of the elevations almost classical in its proportions and balance, and the most satisfying. The even rhythm of bays is interrupted by the projecting portal which consists of a recessed Romanesque doorway set in a Perpendicular surround with gable and corner turrets. Considering it is the main entrance to the cathedral, the portal is modest in size and restrained in design, especially when compared to such exuberant late Romanesque work as Bishop le Puiset's great doorway in the castle. The oak door is nowadays deprived of its famous 12th century sanctuary knocker (so called because criminals seeking sanctuary in the cathedral used it), a stylised lion's head in cast bronze and, according to Pevsner, "one of the greatest examples of the power which the Romanesque style could achieve by stylisation".[1] The conservationists have had their way: the original has been moved to the Cathedral Treasury and a replica fixed to the door.

The head-on view from Palace Green verges on the classical, with the dominant crossing tower and north transept at the centre flanked by the balancing if not quite symmetrical masses of the west towers and east transept. The north transept, however, fails to provide the strength needed to give visual support to the crossing tower because it is acutely lopsided. No attempt has been made to disguise the fact that the east aisle of the transept has a much lower roof than the rest, or that the turrets flanking the 13th century gable are different in shape and size. The arrangement in the south transept is essentially the same, but the lopsided effect is largely obscured by the Chapter House and monastery buildings.

Before entering the cathedral there is one other part of the exterior which needs to be considered, difficult though it is to view at close quarters because of the sharp fall in the ground. This is the mid-13th century east transept, a wonderfully robust piece of Early English architecture, which replaced the Romanesque apsidal east end. We are told that James Wyatt spoiled it by excessive restoration, but it is still very fine. It is remarkable for its great width which adds a whole new dimension to the cathedral. Previously the eastward thrust of nave and aisles was merely rounded off with three apses. Now the east-west axis was effectively challenged by a new cross-axis of secondary importance to that of the main transepts, but far more powerful and unified in its external treatment which consisted of a central rose flanked by lancet windows set between buttresses and framed by almost free-standing corner turrets - a cluster of highly articulated vertical elements, alternately deeply recessed and boldly projecting, whose effect stands in complete contrast to the flat Romanesque treatment of the north and south sides of the cathedral. On the gable-ended north front, which was built last, the treatment was modified, inspired, Pevsner suggests, by the east window of the Angel Choir at Lincoln, put in about 1275.[2] The enormous Joseph window, with its graceful tracery, fills the whole space between corner turrets and provides just the simplicity and strength which is lacking in the main transept.

It can be argued that none of this matters very much when the building "has about it", as Conant says, "the air of serene finality which belongs of right to the greatest masterpieces".[3] To grumble about shortcomings is like the music critic who singles out a Beethoven symphony for its facile harmonies and unsubtle rhythms. Certainly the critic at Durham is silenced once inside the cathedral, overawed by the greatness of the vision and dazzled by the technical prowess. The inside of a cathedral matters more than the outside and medieval churches were conceived from inside out, which is incidentally what attracted the architects of the Modern Movement, more intent on plan and section than on elevation, to medieval rather than to classical architecture. In fact, as soon as we are inside, we become preoccupied with plan and section, and of course with space, which is the result of plan and section combined.

If it was my love of Romanesque architecture which originally took me to Durham, the first experience of the nave would have more than made up for any disappointment I might have felt with the exterior. The most striking quality is an overwhelming sense of unity, due above all to the fact that the whole of the interior is roofed with quadripartite ribbed stone vaulting which looks all of a piece even though the vaulting of the chancel is a 13th century reconstruction after the structural failure of the original vaulting. Indeed seen from the inside, most of cathedral is of a piece, nave, chancel, transept and aisles all having been built in a mere forty years, between 1093 and 1133.

The rhythm in the nave and chancel is slow and solemn as befits the shrine of the great St Cuthbert. This is because the more usual arrangement of having every pier the same and every bay carrying one vaulted compartment is here replaced by a double-bay system of primary piers, with clusters of shafts attached, alternating with simple round secondary piers. The primary piers relate to the primary structure of transverse arches and, between these, a double compartment of quadripartite rib vaulting which takes its support off corbels or short shafts rising from the gallery shelf. This is so at least up to the crossing, where an additional tall shaft provides the support and that continuous slender line which enables the eye to distinguish between structure and infill, or, to draw yet another parallel with modern architecture, between frame and panel. In the chancel additonal shafts are the rule, and the principle of separating structure from infill is reinforced by the use of transverse arches between every bay, which quickens the rhythm, perhaps appropriately as we approach the shrine of St Cuthbert.

Although the emphasis is on the primary piers, with their tall triple shafts supporting the triple transverse arches spanning the nave, the bold cylindrical form of the secondary piers, which do more than provide every other support to the longitudinal arcades dividing the nave from the aisles, repeatedly draws the eye to them, making them by far the most memorable feature of the cathedral. This is due in no small measure to the extraordinary decoration of fluting, chevron, spiral or lozenge, all large-scale, naive and coarse, but a wonderful celebration of the column's prodigious rotundity

It is of course very moving to know that the vaults of the chancel aisles are the very first quadripartite ribbed vaults anywhere and that in this masterpiece of Romanesque architecture, therefore, are sown the seeds of Gothic. It is no accident, moreover, that the Gothic style developed in the darker northern light where large windows were an advantage. Just as quadripartite vaulting made it possible to have the full clerestory lighting which the tunnel vaults current in southern France would not permit, so very large panels of window became feasible once it was discovered how to transmit to the ground the forces generated by the transverse arches and ribbed vaults through a frame of shafts, piers and buttresses. At Durham we are not aware of the flying buttresses because these are concealed inside the galleries of the nave, but we observe unfailingly that the transverse arches are mostly pointed in the Gothic manner and that they continue the long vertical line of the shafts which support them. What is so wonderful about Durham is that, having observed the Gothic style as it were in embryo in the Romanesque part of the cathedral, we can then move to the east transept, the Chapel of the Nine Altars, and appreciate it in its mature form, not only in the relentless alternation of buttress and lancet, but in the north wall which is entirely window.

The east transept is so called because of its great width which makes it project well beyond the chancel aisles and gives its plan form the character of a transept. It was built in fact to accommodate more altars - hence its other name of Chapel of the Nine Altars - because the three altars in the apse which terminated the Romanesque chancel and chancel aisles were insufficient for a thriving monastery. It is unusual if not quite unique, the only other example in England being the east end of Fountains Abbey which just preceded and clearly inspired it. The first thing we notice is that the floor level is some six feet lower than the chancel floor and we must presume that the master mason, Richard Farnham, took advantage of the natural fall in the ground to gain height and so add to the drama of repeated verticals in the form of buttresses, piers and a multitude of slender shafts. The width of the transept is divided into three unequal bays by large buttresses, the central bay being narrower to make it precisely the same width as the Romanesque chancel, thus relating the new work to the old. It is all the more surprising, therefore, that the outer bays bear no relation to the width of the chancel aisles, so that the builders of the east transept had to resort to sexpartite vaulting with transverse ribs set askew. This is just one instance where vaulting problems remained unresolved. Other instances are in the west towers and in the main transepts where projecting corner turrets containing vices prevent one of the four vault ribs from being completed.

The unique and brilliant vault over the central bay of the east transept more than makes up for any minor failings elsewhere. Instead of single ribs springing from the piers in the four corners, there are twin ribs which separate to form eight ribs and to butt into a large ring at the crown incorporating wonderfully carved seated figures of the four Evangelists. Wyatt's rose window, much decried by art historians, is effectively contained by this vault and looks well enough when seen fron the nave over the Gilbert Scott and Neville screens, but appears two-dimensional and weak close to and by the side of the deeply set lancets or Joseph window with its astonishing double layer of tracery.

There remains the Galilee Chapel at the west end, started by Bishop le Puiset soon after 1170. If it were not such an exquisite interior space, we would be right to condemn it as an aberration. Wyatt must have thought it so since he was only just stopped from demolishing it. It was built on such steeply sloping ground that it had to be propped up with new foundations and buttresses 250 years later; it managed to obscure the important west front of the cathedral from the bottom of the great west window down to the ground; and it encouraged the closure and mutilation of the west portal when in the early 15th century Cardinal Langely erected there a monument to himself. We are told, moreover, that le Puiset built the Galilee Chapel especially for women to prevent them from entering the eastern parts of his church. The still Romanesque interior is indeed feminine in its lightness and delicacy, standing in complete and fascinating contrast to the rest of the cathedral. The effect must have been even lighter when each support consisted only of two Purbeck columns with a gap between, instead of the solid cluster which we now see and which was the result of strengthening the supports by the addition of two sandstone columns.

The column clusters carry semi-circular arches and divide the Galilee Chapel into five equal aisles, of which the middle three have higher ceilings and, together with Cardinal Langley's monument at the end of the centre aisle, are the only features which give any sense of hierarchy or orientation. The chapel is in fact wider than it is long, so that looking across its full width we see the receding planes of arches and columns and could almost imagine ourselves in the hypostyle hall of a mosque. The arches have triple bands of chevron decoration, or what in French is called more descriptively, as Clapham points out, "baton brisé, indicating that it consists of the breaking of the mouldings of an arch or string course into a zig-zag".[4] The greatest surprise of the Galilee Chapel is that such a beautiful and sophisticated supporting structure should be roofed in timber where the rest of the cathedral is vaulted in stone. The bays are square and we can imagine the dazzling effect of transverse arches with chevron decoration carried on, and playful rib vaults suspended between.

Durham is the only example in England of a Romanesque cathedral in which the sense of unity is overwhelming. This is because Durham, of all the post-conquest cathedrals, was started late as a result of which it was vaulted throughout and perhaps more expertly built. It did not suffer changes and additions to anything like the same extent as many of the other post-conquest cathedrals which were started earlier, like Canterbury, Winchester or Gloucester. In addition to the vaulting, about which I have said enough, two other features make important contributions to this sense of unity. The continuity and consistency, as well as the pleasing proportions, of arcade, gallery and clerestory in the nave, chancel and transepts;

and the continuity and consistency of the superbly decorative and monumental interlaced blind arcading on the outer walls of the aisles and transepts.

I cannot conclude without some reference to the grandeur of the post-conquest cathedrals. After the Saxon churches these represented a vast and definitive increase in size and scale. There was absolutely nothing provincial or insular about these cathedrals, and later Gothic rebuilding was often placed on the foundations of the Romanesque work, as in the case of the Perpendicular nave at Canterbury, which made use of Lanfranc's foundations. English architecture only became provincial at the Renaissance. Grander than most, Durham cathedral is extraordinary because it was at the fringes of an empire where not even the Romans had built so magnificently. Durham, now with its 900 years worn so lightly, was indeed built for eternity.

6 The Artists' Response:
Images of Durham Cathedral from c.1780

Rosalind Billingham

In 1833 the Durham-born painter George Fennel Robson died. From accounts of his life, during which he rose to be president of the Old Watercolour Society in London, it is clear that he was remembered for two things. Firstly he had no formal training, but, having received basic tuition in Durham, learned much by watching other artists paint his native city. Secondly, the image of Durham Cathedral recurred with sufficient frequency at the Old Watercolour Society's exhibition for it to be impressed on the memory of regular visitors to the annual shows.[1] Not unnaturally, Robson included Durham among the prints in *Picturesque Views of the English Cities* edited by John Britton and published in 1828. The example well illustrates the way in which the image of the cathedral became known before the advent of photography.

Most of the outstanding watercolour artists worked in Durham at some time between c.1783 and c.1810, the period when this peculiarly English art reached its peak. Robson, as a child, could certainly have seen some of its most distinguished practitioners at work, including J.M.W. Turner and Thomas Girtin. By c.1780 English topographical artists were beginning to travel far more widely in their own country. This was partly due to improved roads at home and political instability abroad. Drawings were needed for volumes of prints, which were becoming increasingly popular, and a new source of employment was emerging. A typical early sample of this kind of project is Paul Sandby's *Collection of 150 Select Views in England, Wales, Scotland and Ireland*, published in 1783. In this particular volume the Durham plate is not good, so presumably Sandby was poorly served by his engraver.

Two far more lively images of the same period are preserved at the Victoria and Albert Museum. One is by Thomas Hearne, dated 1783, the other by Edward Edwards five years later (Figs. 49, 50). Hearne was best known for his work on *The Antiquities of Britain* published in 1807. Early in his career Edwards was employed as a trainee scene painter in Newcastle. A friend of Paul Sandby's, Edwards became Professor of Perspective at the Royal Academy in 1788, the year in which he drew Durham. Both produced drawings which are interesting because of what they tell us about the building history of the cathedral.[2] Hearne shows the western towers without pinnacles; Edwards shows them added to the north-western tower, and records scaffolding on the south-western one for the addition of this feature. Both artists use rather contrived foregrounds as was the custom in the late 18th century; verisimilitude in this matter was not required. Samuel Hiéronymus Grimm also rendered this scene.

Sketching tours were sometimes undertaken with the support of the landed gentry. Cotman's visit to Durham in 1805, when he was staying with the Cholmeleys at Brandsby in Yorkshire, is an example of friendly and enlightened patronage which is well documented, and from 1808 J.M.W. Turner received similar support from Walter Fawkes of Farnley Hall near Leeds. Some connoisseurs such as Dr. Thomas Monro, who employed both Turner and Girtin, collected watercolours, while between 1826 and 1828, Mrs. George Haldimand employed G.F. Robson to acquire watercolours for her. This became an important collection.

Fig. 49 Durham Cathedral, watercolour by Thomas Hearne, 1783

Fig. 50 Durham Cathedral, watercolour by Edward Edwards, 1788

Fig. 51 Durham Cathedral and Bridge, watercolour by Thomas Girtin, 1799

Fig. 52 Durham Cathedral from the Bridge, watercolour by J.M.W. Turner, c. 1798

Fig. 53 Durham Castle and Cathedral, watercolour by Thomas Girtin, 1799

Fig. 54 Durham Castle and Cathedral, watercolour by John Sell Cotman, c. 1809-10

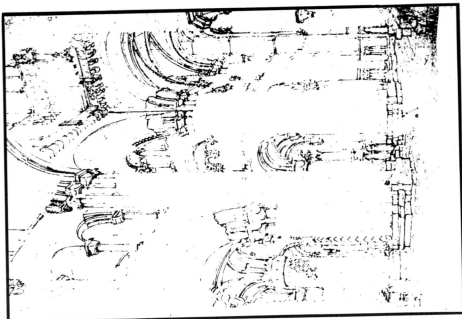

Fig. 56 Drawing from Tweed and Lakes Sketchbook, by
J.M.W. Turner,1797

Fig. 55 Drawing from Tweed and Lakes Sketchbook, by
J.M.W. Turner,1797

Thomas Girtin first visited Durham in 1796 and a drawing he did on the spot from a point below Framwellgate Bridge has survived in the collection of the Museum of Fine Arts in Boston, U.S.A. Turner did a drawing from the almost identical place when he visited the city a year later. It survives in the Tweed and Lakes sketchbook, which is part of the Turner Bequest housed at the Tate Gallery. The sketches of both artists are line drawings in pencil, and it is fascinating to compare the way in which they worked them up in the studio. Girtin's picture, now in the Whitworth Art Galley, Manchester, was completed in 1799 (Fig.51). Turner's is now in the Royal Academy and it is datable to c.1798 (Fig. 52, cf. Fig.5). Both these watercolours represent a pinnacle of topographical illustration; when Turner moved beyond this, it was to something quite without parallel in the rendering of a sense of place, and for Girtin, it represents a turning point in his career.

The two artists have chosen basically different light effects, Turner achieving the greater sense of space, with the cathedral pale above the dark bridge. Girtin chose to paint the bridge light, with part of the cathedral tinted with a golden glow. This, though a fairly accurate rendering of some of Durham's most poetic light effects, was an aspect of Girtin's style which Turner much envied; he admired what he called Girtin's "golden paintings". Nevertheless, he achieved the greater sense of three dimensional volume.

Turner drew his version for the portrait painter John Hoppner, R.A. This is recorded by the watercolour painter Joseph Farington, who himself draw Durham Cathedral during a tour of the North in 1801. His diaries give invaluable source material for the study of Turner and his contemporaries. On October 24th 1798 he noted that Turner had offered to make a drawing for him from a subject in his sketchbooks. He had paid Hoppner the same compliment and "Hoppner", he said, "had chosen a subject at Durham".[3]

Girtin's early death in 1802 prompted Turner to make the legendary remark that "if Girtin had lived, I should have starved". Prior to 1802, Turner was not earning his living by his experiments in oil painting, and by the last years of Girtin's life, the two artists were rivals in the art of topographical landscape. Girtin's development can be traced through several paintings of Durham Cathedral. The earliest picture of 1795 at the Laing Gallery, Newcastle, predates Girtin's visit to Durham and was copied from a watercolour by the architectural topographer Edward Dayes. Dayes taught Girtin, and the painting he studied is now in the Yale Centre for British Art. It is from such works that Girtin learned such "picturesque" devices as the little boat seen also in another early work in the British Museum, where the view of the cathedral is approximately that from Prebends' Bridge. In this work the cathedral is far more convincing and represents a development from the Laing painting. The trees, too, are more naturalistic, but in neither case does the surrounding landscape relate particularly closely to the Durham peninsula.

The two paintings produced after 1796 show how his eyes were opened by seeing the city. By the time Girtin came to paint the Whitworth picture in 1799, he had perfected his mastery of architectural draughtsmanship by making copies after the Italian masters Piranesi and Canaletto. The very beautiful rendering of the cathedral carries the conviction that direct observation brings with it. Here Girtin has almost escaped from picturesque conventions. However, the men in a boat re-appear on the right-hand side as a visual stop, because he, unlike Turner, had decided to omit the building at the end of Framwellgate Bridge on the right hand side. Turner, having darkened the bridge, uses this shape to compose the edge without need of further contrivance. He also paints the water with the ruffled surface of a flowing river while still indicating the reflections of the cathedral; Girtin's water, on the other hand, is motionless, and no water flows over the weir.

Girtin's painting in the Victoria and Albert Museum shows some of the same characteristics (Fig. 53). It is based on a drawing in the Hickman Baron Collection and the view can be located exactly today as the view from Framwellgate Waterside, below the National Savings building. If the tower seems a little wide, and the architectural detail is not stressed, the cathedral nevertheless dominates as it should, and the picture still conveys a strong impression of this part of Durham, even though the foreground buildings on the left have not survived (see Fig.4).

The third major watercolourist of the early 19th century to paint Durham from below Framwellgate Bridge was John Sell Cotman, who worked up the painting now in the Norwich Castle Museum from sketches made during his visit to the city in 1805 (Fig.54). It is not exactly comparable because it is proportionately broader than Turner's and Girtin's works, and it is thus less focused on the cathedral. This will be discussed below with other products of Cotman's 1805 visit.

Meanwhile Turner had worked up a magnificent representation of the interior of the cathedral from page twelve of the sketchbook used on the 1797 visit and now in the Turner Bequest (Fig.55). It is of special interest, because here we can follow the way Britain's greatest 19th century painter reacted to one of her most impressive buildings. This drawing is a technical *tour de force*. Turner seems to have been drawing from a point by the wall of the South aisle approximately level with the chevron pillar, but it is not possible to see as much of the cathedral as this without turning the head quite markedly from side to side. Architectural drawing techniques are normally based on the convention of a single viewpoint, but here Turner handled the problem of a two point perspective with the dexterity of the true virtuoso. On page ten of the same sketch book there is a magnificent drawing of the crossing (Fig.56) and on page thirteen another of the south choir aisle looking west to what is now the St. Oswald window, but which then still contained Gothic tracery. (This was removed in the Victorian period when the windows were restored to their Romanesque form).[4] In this drawing, he has made a careful drawing of the composite column to the west of the Neville tomb.

Because Turner has, in the finished watercolour, expressed the volumes and the play of light against dark forms that are part of Durham's glory, the viewer does not question that this is, in some real sense, a true image of the cathedral (Pl.VI). In fact, Turner has taken liberties with the architecture. He has not only omitted the screen at the entrance to the south choir aisle, and suppressed details of the vaulting in the interests of lighting, as Ian Warrell and Diane Perkins have pointed out.[5] He has also altered the composite and cylindrical pillars, so that the foreground pillar is composite rather than cylindrical. Readers will remember that at Durham the composite piers take the weight of the supporting arches of the high vault. They alternate with the cylindrical, ornamented pillars. Composite piers support the crossing. Turner, by changing the pillars round, created something architecturally illogical, but artistically convincing.

Fig. 57 Durham Cathedral, watercolour by J.M.W. Turner, c. 1835

Fig. 58 Durham Cathedral, watercolour by William Daniell, 1805

Fig. 59 Durham Cathedral from the River, watercolour by John Pearson, undated

Fig. 60 Durham Cathedral and Castle, watercolour by G.F. Robson, undated

Fig. 61 Durham Cathedral from Prebends' Bridge, watercolour by G.F. Robson, undated

Fig. 62 Durham, oil on canvas by J.W. Carmichael, 1841

It is difficult to decide to what extent Turner consciously intended to make the cathedral more Gothic in its porportions. Partly this is due to perspective convention. In a cathedral, the viewer normally changes his viewpoint between looking at the vault and the base of a pillar. It is a perceptual fact that, if a draughtsman does this, he will elongate his subject. But Turner had probably been influenced by the Gothic taste of the late 18th century. He deliberately suppressed the decoration of the cylindrical pier; perhaps because at the time he painted this, Norman architecture was not widely appreciated and the boldly incised pillars were doubtless regarded as barbaric.

Turner's best known watercolour of Durham, painted c.1835 and now in the National Gallery of Scotland, is an image of pure poetry (Fig.57). He makes no attempt at architectural or topographical exactitude, any more than he did in his other mature cathedral paintings, of Salisbury and Ely, for example. But it is a portrait of Durham that reveals both its poetry and its drama. If he has slimmed down the west towers, he has made them soar, and if he has turned the west front at an impossible angle to the river, he has stressed the way in which the cathedral dominates the surrounding landscape. This watercolour is also evidence of Turner's prodigious memory. We know that he was in Durham in 1801, at the time of a journey to Edinburgh, because there are two rapid sketches in the Helmsley notebook of the cathedral and castle, one with a rainbow, and a darker silhouette made a few minutes later. A more finished version of part of this view depicted the cathedral only. This coolly beautiful study is now in the National Gallery of Scotland and is less known than most of Turner's Durham studies, because it is so close-toned and hard to reproduce.

The next time Turner was certainly in Durham was in the Autumn of 1817, when he was taking notes for illustrations to Surtees *History of Durham*. This led to finished watercolours of Gibside and Hylton and Raby castles but not of Durham itself, though there are a number of sketches on the City in the Durham North Shore Sketchbook, which he was using at the time. His beautifully free colour study of the cathedral with a rainbow in the Turner Bequest was probably carried out at this time, but there is no evidence of Turner having been in the city after that date. The finished watercolour has been drawn from memory with, it would seem, no detailed studies of the cathedral from the river drawn after 1797, and no visit more recent than 1817. It is presumed that Turner worked up his image around 1835 because W. Miller engraved it the following year. If this is so, the towering impression of the cathedral had lingered in this memory for eighteen years.

Meanwhile, Cotman's visit to Durham in 1805 had resulted in some pictures which were both poetic and accurate. It is now evident from the archive of the Cholmeley family, his friends and patrons at Brandsby Hall, that he did not visit Durham until 1805 and, even then, he did not particularly want to, because he was more interested in painting trees. Indeed he eventually painted Prebends' Bridge, or as he called it The New Bridge at Durham, framed by woodland, in 1808.

Cotman was in the city by 4th September 1805 and wrote to Francis Cholmeley from Shotton's Inn two days later "Durham is a delightfully situated City". Later he commented that he found the cathedral "magnificent tho' not so fine as York", a view that many late 20th century critics might wish to reverse, but which was entirely in line with the taste of his time.

The finest of his 1805 cathedral views was undoubtedly that from the south-west, and it is arguably the greatest of all the topographical drawings of the cathedral (Pl.VII). The detail is remarkably accurate, and the compositional planning of the light and dark areas has an architectonic quality worthy of its subject. Cotman had studied the cathedral of his own native Norwich, and was used to Norman architecture: it is interesting that one of his watercolours survives of a Norwich pillar with similar decorations to that of the pillars of the Durham transepts. Of the Durham picture, Laurence Binyon, author of *For the Fallen*, wrote "It has Girtin's largeness and serious simplicity, and, at the same time, a deeper comprehension of the grandeur of the architecture [and] an intense feeling for the actual moulding and essential character of the old stone".[6]

The other watercolour developed from the 1805 drawings is the one in the Norwich Castle Museum mentioned above. Two related studies survive, but neither shows the same composition. A very simplified watercolour showing the cathedral and only a small part of the castle survives in the Tate Gallery. It is taken from a lower viewpoint than the finished picture, and is compositionally less satisfactory. A rather rubbed drawing survives in the British Museum taken from further above the river. In 20th century terms it approximates to the view from Durham station (the viaduct was not built until 1857), but the artist was probably not so high up. The finished picture constructed from these studies is a fine evocation of the old city, with dramatic contrasts of light and dark, and a magnificently stylised waterfall in the foreground. But, in spite of all these qualities, it does not tell us as much about the cathedral as the British Museum watercolour.

Cotman, Turner and Girtin were the most outstanding of a large number of artists who were engaged in similar activity, and one or two artists who have left us fine representations of Durham may be taken to represent the others. William Daniell has left us a strong, dark-toned image of the cathedral from Prebends' Bridge (Fig.58). Like Cotman, he aimed to be accurate, and largely succeeded, though we may reasonably wonder whether this particular part of the Wear was ever used as a watering place. Another dramatic view with particularly felicitous colouring by John Pearson is also preserved at the Victoria and Albert Museum (Fig.59). Again the architecture is observed with loving detail, but this work is not by the Durham watercolourist who was the father of John Loughborough Pearson (see below) because he died four years before J.L. Pearson was born. Little has been recorded about the earlier John Pearson, but he was clearly a practitioner of skill and poetry.

If most of the pioneer sketching tours in which artists explored and recorded their own country had been completed by c.1810, the market for watercolours and prints developed considerably while interested collectors were prevented from travelling on the Continent during the Napoleonic Wars. The expansion continued during the next few years, and large numbers of watercolour drawings and prints of that period can be found of most of the English cathedral cities

It was inevitable that clichés developed during such proliferation of images, but it is interesting to see how artists coped with the increased demand. George Fennel Robson produced some intriguing views of Durham. He is generally considered to have been influenced stylistically by John Varley, one of the founder members of the Old Watercolour Society, who himself exhibited Durham subjects there in 1813 and 1825. As one might expect from a native on the city, Robson selected some surprising and unhackneyed view points. In a painting in the Victoria and Albert Museum, the cathedral is seen from Flass Vale before the building of the viaduct (Fig.60). A slightly different view was engraved by E.J. Findon in 1832. The Vale is now overgrown, but Robson's view tallies extremely closely with a photograph, c.1944, which shows that this rural scene is topographically correct.[7] The same accuracy characterises Robson's more familiar views, although the compositions may have a distinctive 'twist'. Thus, his painting from Prebends' Bridge (Fig.61) has a foreground of stonemasons leisurely completing the parapet of the bridge. (The new bridge was built ten years before Robson was born). His painting of the cathedral from the opposite direction makes use of an arch of Framwellgate Bridge to frame the building, a view which can only be appreciated from a boat. It is interesting that Edward Dayes had drawn a similar view, dated 1797, which is now in the Ashmolean Museum. A more distant south-western view is shown

Fig. 63 Durham Cathedral, West View, engraving after R.W. Billings, 1846

in a detailed study of the cathedral Robson painted in 1809. His vantage point has, since 1841, been known as Observatory Hill, and the scene depicted is essentially that existing today (cf Fig.2). J.W. Carmichael, a Newcastle-born artist best known for his marine paintings, painted a similar view, and there is a closely related engraving of this (Fig.62).

Two artists who recorded Durham for engraving projects in the early Victorian period are noteworthy. One was Thomas Allom, a landscape painter and founder member of the Royal Institute of British Architects, who contributed drawings of the cathedral to *Durham and Northumberland Illustrated*, published by Thomas Rose in 1847. He drew amongst others, the views from Framwellgate Bridge and Prebends' Bridge which had, by this time, become standard. But by far the most important print maker, as far as Durham is concerned, was Robert William Billings, who was a polymath, practising as a draughtsman, engraver, publisher, architect and sculptor. His *Architectural Illustrations and Descriptions of the Cathedral Church of Durham* of 1843 was published in London by T. and W. Boone. This is the most comprehensive set of images of our subject that was captable of wide reproduction until the invention of photogravure at the end of the 19th century. It may be argued that the very quantity of information held by the plates limits their value as creative interpretations, but as an architectural source of reference, this collection was unrivalled. Apart from conventional studies of the interior and exterior, there are a number of interesting plates of details including the carving above the south door of the nave, the panelling in the tower and half elevations of the east side of the Neville Screen. In all there are over 70 plates, and it is not surprising that Billings enjoyed a considerable reputation as an architectural draughtsman. He produced several other prints of the cathedral in its landscape setting where his artistic personality comes through more strongly. The silvery grace of 'Durham Cathedral: West View', published by George Andrews of Durham in 1846, is a good example of his work (Fig.63).

One surviving etching of the cathedral has curiosity value, that produced by the young John Loughborough Pearson in 1835. A copy survives in the University Library. Pearson ended his career by designing Truro Cathedral, a late exercise in Revivalist Gothic. While it cannot be said to have any direct relationship to Durham, the design of Truro shows a thorough knowledge of the medieval tradition. It is interesting that Pearson was articled to the Durham architect Ignatius Bonomi before he left the North East to practise in London.

An unusual traveller's record is preserved in the Prussian State Library in Berlin. In 1829 Felix Mendelssohn visited Durham during a journey to Scotland which he immortalised by writing the 'Fingal's Cave' overture. He drew the cathedral from memory, presumably having viewed it from South Street and the River Banks (Pl.VIII). Ready-made paints in tubes and pans which led to the fashion for sketching in the later 19th century were not available as early as this, and the professional artist's equipment was heavy and cumbersome. Although this image was obviously worked up from memory, his impression of the cathedral is not too wildly inaccurate, but the surrounding buildings belong to a Baroque city of central Europe, rather than to northern England. What impressed him was the drama of the gorge, and, in particular, the role played by the trees.

As the 19th century progressed, painters saw the cathedral in a changing environment, and in some cases quite literally, a different light. Alfred William Hunt painted the view from a point above Elvet Bridge: here, for the first time the cathedral dominates a slightly smokey Victorian town. By the time John Varley, a descendant of his more famous painter grandfather,

Fig. 64 Above the Rooftops, watercolour by Thomas Greenhalgh, 1884

Fig. 65 The Galilee, Evening, charcoal by Dennis Creffield, 1987

Fig. 66 The Central Tower, Durham Cathedral, charcoal by Dennis Creffield, 1987

saw Durham, domestic buildings rather than the cathedral dominated his consciousness, and the foreground is better observed than the historic citadel.[8] Varley saw Durham from the railway station, a view which had been newly opened up, and which has since become one of the most famous. Good watercolour records of this panorama include those by Thomas Greenhalgh (1884) and Mary Davison (1891), the former being illustrated here (Fig.64, cf Fig.3).

It is unsurprising that there are few portraits of Durham dating from the first half of the 20th century. In addition to competition from photographers, the two World Wars stunted this kind of artistic activity, and the period between 1919 and 1939 was the time of the greatest suffering and deprivation that the North East had known. This led to the area receiving a bad press. J.B. Priestley, for example, never even mentions the cathedral in his *English Journey*,

Fig. 67 A Beam, charcoal by Virginia Bodman, 1983

which records a journey round the country in 1933. He refers only to the view from the railway - "the fine grim aspect of the city of Durham, with that baleful dark hulk of castle which, at a distance makes the city look like some place in a Gothic tale of blood and terror"[9] - because his main purpose was to bring the reader's attention the appalling plight of the people during the inter-war recession.

There are art-historical reasons, as well, for the dearth of topographical pictures. Landscape artists were too busy absorbing, or attempting to absorb the lessons of European Modernism, of Surrealism and Abstraction, and it is only more recently that a number of artists have become interested in the possibilities of finding a contemporary language to render a sense of place. Of these, Dennis Creffield affords a link with the past. In 1987, he, like the 19 th century artists, travelled round the country, and having the advantage of modern transport, interpreted all twenty-six of the English medieval cathedrals, producing large scale charcoal drawings. He has recalled, "Each day I drew them - each night I slept in their shadow - and their shapes filled my dreams". Of Durham he wrote "Probably the best loved cathedral in England. Its spectacular position - situated on its rock high above the river, and its massive and noble interior make it every man's idea of Norman architecture." By his own confession he found it difficult to draw, but be achieved some very unusual renderings of the towers, and a most evocative interior view of the Galilee which clearly caught his imagination (Figs. 65, 66). He has written, "I drew inside the Galilee Chapel as it was growing dark. The Mystery Plays were being performed and I could hear the shouts of the players in the distance". He is the only one of the artists discussed who has written openly about his christian beliefs, and he has quoted

Wittgenstein's remark that "architecture immortalises and glorifies something. Hence there can be no architecture where there is nothing to glorify", and about the cathedral drawings he commented, "These drawings are my glory to their glory which came from the glory of God".[10]

Creffield is not the only artist to appreciate the value of charcoal in rendering architectural experience. It is a medium through which fleeting impressions can be recorded rapidly; it also has expressive possibilities which have been more fully realised since the German Expressionists, as the individual gesture of the hand can be recorded easily. Two former Artists in Residence, who have worked at the cathedral under a scheme which has been operating since 1983, have produced powerful work in charcoal: Matthew Carey and Virginia Bodman. The drawings by the latter are particularly interesting, because, daunted by interpreting the splendours below, she gained access to the roof and produced a series of drawings, one of which is reproduced here (Fig.67). In the roof space she found medieval debris that had been left deliberately at strategic points to weigh down the vault and stop it springing apart. This became a metaphor for her own interior space, and she used the idea later in a series of semi-abstract paintings, one of which was called 'Emotional Debris'.

Another attempt to render an experience of the cathedral abstractly was that by Maureen Enright who, while a mature student at Coventry Polytechnic, experimented with various visual languages in a whole series of paintings to express this. In 1983 she wrote "I am not concerned with a topographical likeness, but merely with an attempt to comprehend, and perhaps come to terms with, the strange awe-inspiring emotion that persistently takes control every time I enter the cathedral".[11] Difficulties about what abstract paintings communicate to the viewer are central to the whole tradition of European and American Modernism. But Ms. Enright was also interested in Turner, and in her painting 'Cathedral' (Pl.IX) she has produced a work within an iconographic tradition of luminescence which is probably best exemplified in John Piper's Baptistery window at Coventry Cathedral, which is very close to where she was working. There is a sense in her painting of architectural forms bringing their own enlightenment.

In Robert Soden's painting 'God's Factory at Night' the title is more problematic than the image (Pl.X). Few render the exclusively Gothic parts of the cathedral, but Soden chose to draw the East end during restoration when the noise and paraphernalia of the construction industry resembled a factory and was a central feature of the scene. The grid of the temporary scaffolding gives the work a semi-abstract appearance, but the view remains totally recognisable.

Birtley Aris has probably created a more extensive series of images of the cathedral than anyone since Robert Billings. Born in Sunderland, Aris has known Durham from an early age. He has frequently chosen dramatic perspectives looking down from the triforium and clerestory, which are all the more remarkable because they were mainly painted *in situ* with very little studio retouching (Figs.68, 69). These unusual views have, on the one hand, allowed him to avoid cliché, and, on the other, direct comparison with Turner. Aris has been particularly interested in the perspectives visible near the crossing, and has chosen to study them on dull days when "there is a build up of rich shadow made more complex by the relatively limited source of light from clerestory windows and side aisles". This helped him to convey something of the cathedral's mystery. He has written, "Working in this great building was an enriching experience...I became increasingly aware of the enormous time span encompassed by the life of the cathedral...My record will only be a tiny part of its history".[12]

Fig. 69 The Screen and Choir from the North Transept
Clerestory, watercolour by Birtley Aris, 1987

Fig. 68 The Screen from the Triforium in the North Transept,
watercolour by Birtley Aris, 1987

Colin Wilborn has given a new meaning to the phrase "a literal interpretation" because he is interested in recycling material. His large stone sculpture 'Kathedra' (Fig. 70), here photographed in the mason's yard, where the visual link becomes clearer, is now sited on the river bank north of Prebends' Bridge. It is partly made from masonry removed from the cathedral during restoration work. The rest is fashioned from stone from the Dunhouse quarry near Staindrop, which is used by the Durham masons today. It is based on the idea of the Kathedra, or bishop's throne, from which the word cathedral is derived; hence the front of the sculpture is an imposing seat. At the back is a mass of tumbled stone gargoyles. All are different and none are direct copies of cathedral carvings, yet a medieval quality is pervasive. Wilbourn has explained, "What I've ended up with is a metaphor of the cathedral, where on the one side you can find a sense of reason, and on the other is all the confusion and uncertainty of the world".[13]

The other piece he created during his residency was made from part of the cathedral belfry, from oak beams which were removed in the 1980s during restoration. He called it 'The Last Supper Table' and it folds out to reveal a symbolic design worked in marquetry. He explained that he wanted to show how a private occasion, the Last Supper, opened out to become a public event. The work is a conceptual link with 'The Upper Room', thirteen elm trees carved to represent the place of the Last Supper, an environmental work in the woods near Prebends' Bridge. It has won popular acceptance and admiration. It has no direct visual link with the cathedral but, in its evocation of Christian spirituality it is arguably nearer to it in spirit than his other works. Amongst these is 'In the Shadows of the Past' created for the 1990 Gateshead Garden Festival which included a carving of Bishop Carileph (Calais), standing in the shadow of the cathedral he had founded. This work is now permanently sited at Durham University's Botanic Garden in Hollingside Lane.

Wilbourn's sculptures are certainly one of the successes of the Artists in Residence scheme which started at the cathedral in 1983 "to provide time and space for the artist, free of other pressures, so that she or he may respond to the cathedral as a powerful creative statement".[14] No organisation can ensure creativity, but the residency is well-known in the art-world, and has given rise to some striking images.

As a student, Wilbourn was taught by Fenwick Lawson, a Durham-based artist who has produced a remarkable series of sculptures expressing religious themes. Most notable from our point of view is his 'Cuthbert of Farne', which depicts the saint as contemplative rather than bishop (Fig. 71). It was carved from a dying elm tree which grew at the north entrance to the cathedral, and now stands in the cathedral cloister. The grain of the wood evokes both Celtic spirituality and the Farne environment, the latter including an eider duck - still known locally as 'Cuddy's duck', ie. Cuthbert's - nestling in sanctuary at the hermit's feet.

Ultimately it is difficult to gauge the extent of the cathedral's influence on contemporary artists' work. Sometimes a direct reference is acknowledged, as with Marguerite Elliott's 'Tree of Good and Evil' tapestry commissioned for the chapel of St Aidan's College, Durham University. She has stated that the tree "comes from the same forest as the cathedral pillars", though in fact the stone-coloured trunk is not a direct quotation. On the other hand, the impact of the building on the sculptor Dame Elizabeth Frink has been powerful, but imprecise. She is recorded as saying:

"one of my favourite cathedrals is Durham because of the way it's built, its massiveness. I can't recall the carvings there ... I have great difficulty in remembering where I've seen

Fig. 70 Kathedra, sandstone sculpture
by Colin Wilbourn, 1988

Fig. 71 Cuthbert of Farne, wooden
sculpture by Fenwick Lawson, 1983

anything ... I picked Durham because I think it's just a wonderful place. It stands up to anything in Europe ... its columns are amazing. The cut-out patterns on the columns are extraordinary, and how they were made. I can see modern figurative art going in there."[15]

Her remarks highlight the ceaseless inspiration of Durham to artists. Their creativity forges a link with the community which brought the cathedral into being, because the group of monks who settled on the peninsula in AD 995 brought, with St Cuthbert's relics, some of the greatest works of art of the Anglo-Irish school. From then on, throughout the Middle Ages, Durham was woven into the history of art and architecture at the highest level. Though the cathedral lost many of its treasures at the Reformation, and more particularly during the Civil War, it was magnificently furnished after the Restoration. It has been embellished and interpreted up to the present day. The fact that it continues to excite contemporary artists is one of the more satisfying examples of historical continuity.

Acknowledgement

The author wishes to record her thanks for the help and encouragement given by the late Rev. H.W. Langford.

7 The Cathedral and its Monastic Community
Alan J. Piper

The present cathedral was built as a monastic cathedral, the church of a community of Benedictine monks. They formed the cathedral chapter from 1083-1539, and that period of some 450 years saw the creation of the building as it now stands. The monastic cathedral was an institution almost entirely restricted to England. It had developed under the Anglo-Saxons, but it also found favour among several of the early Norman bishops following the Norman Conquest in 1066, and the number of such cathedrals was substantially increased. The bishops involved were themselves monks and so were in a good position to take the place of an abbot as the heads of their monastic communities. Subsequently it became increasingly rare for their successors to be monks, and this, combined with the range of other functions that bishops were expected to fulfil, meant that they ceased to associate closely with their cathedral communities.[1]

The process by which this separation took place gave rise to considerable friction in various ways, prompting definition of the rights and responsibilities of the two sides. While this was certainly the case at Durham, one matter over which there seems to have been no serious conflict was the cathedral building itself. The absence of conflict is probably the reason why it never proved necessary to define the respective roles of the bishop and his cathedral community in respect of the building, its maintenance and enhancement. The absence of conflict does imply, however, that both sides acted in accordance with an understanding of their roles. Whether this understanding was clearly established from the start, or whether it evolved over time, is not entirely clear, but its operation can be discerned both in the history of major building projects and in the regular provision that was made for maintenance.[2]

Durham cathedral's monastic community was established in 1083 by Bishop William of St Calais (1080-96), to replace the congregation of St Cuthbert which had fled from Lindisfarne in 875. The new community was formed by bringing together the twenty-three monks from Jarrow and Wearmouth, where monastic life had been revived during the previous decade. Bishop William was himself a monk, from a house close to the borders of Normandy, and he was second only to Gundulf of Rochester among those bishops who, after the Norman Conquest, added to the number of English cathedrals that were served by monks rather than secular priests.

The monastic historian, Symeon of Durham, writing early in the 12th century, protrayed the changes of 1083 as a restoration of the arrangements established by St Aidan at the foundation of the see on Lindisfarne in 635.[3] Historical precedent apart, Bishop William must certainly have regarded it as decidedly irregular that his cathedral was served by a community of hereditary priests, who had inherited their positions because their forebears had travelled with St Cuthbert's body from Lindisfarne to Chester-le-Street and then, late in the 10th century, to Durham. The bishop must also have been aware that these families had loyalties reaching deep into the Anglo-Saxon past; if Durham and its castle was to be an effective bulwark for the new, Norman, order of things, he could hardly be comfortable with the leading figures of his cathedral representing an alternative allegiance.[4]

The decision to replace the cathedral built by the Anglo-Saxon congregation of St Cuthbert was a natural outcome of the events of 1083; a far more imposing building would show clearly that the changes had been for the better. But there was some delay. In part this may be attributed to the need to provide for the domestic needs of the new monastic community, although it did prove possible to make use of work begun a little earlier by Bishop Walcher (1071-80).[5] Then there were the vicissitudes of Bishop William's career.[6] He was a leading figure during the closing years of William the Conqueror's reign; when the king died in 1087 and his second son, William Rufus, secured the kingdom of England for himself, the new king took Bishop William as his closest adviser. Early in 1088, however, the bishop fell under suspicion of having acquiesced in a rebellion, and went into exile for almost three years; during that time the monks built their refectory. William was restored to his see in September 1091, when the king led an expedition north to repel a Scottish invasion. Within two years, on Friday 29 July 1093, the bishop and the prior together began to dig the foundations for the new building, and on Thursday 11 August the bishop, prior and monks laid the first stones.[7]

Symeon states that it was Bishop William who ordered the old cathedral to be destroyed, and that it was from his own resources that the bishop undertook the building of the new cathedral, with the monks building their domestic quarters. Symeon was also careful to record that in 1083 Bishop William made a division between his possessions and the lands for the monks' food and clothing, also recording that the bishop appointed one of the monks as sacrist, to care for the cathedral and have custody of the body of St Cuthbert.[8] It is perhaps questionable whether such clear definition had in fact been provided on all these matters: Symeon wrote at a time when the monastic community had reason to be apprehensive about the conduct of Bishop Willaims's successor, Ranulf Flambard (1099-1128), and this may have coloured his account. Indeed it may already have become clear that work on the nave was to be financed, not from Bishop Ranulf's own resources, but from offerings. Symeon's successor as chronicler noted that things were not what they had been under Bishop William, when the collections from the church used to go to the monks for their buildings.[9]

The pattern of major building projects being undertaken at the initiative of the bishop appears to have been normal during the 12th and early 13th centuries. The construction of the Galilee at the west end of the cathedral is firmly attributed to Bishop Hugh of Le Puiset (1153-95), and the fuller of the two accounts of his works gives no hint that the bishop did not finance it.[10] The eastern transept, later known as the Chapel of the Nine Altars, was described as the undertaking of Bishop Richard Poore (1228-37); although offerings were encouraged by means of an indulgence freeing contributors from thirty days' penance, this does not exclude the possibility that funds were also provided by the bishop, but he died before work started.[11] After his death it was the prior who began the new work, with the bishop helping, as the monastic chronicler put it,[12] and it was the prior who encouraged contributions by issuing a document that set out the indulgences and other spiritual benefits that benefactors would receive.[13]

These initiatives on the part of the prior may be regarded as symptomatic of a developing trend, an inevitable trend as it seems when seen in retrospect. The prior, as the head of the community that lived beside the cathedral and worshipped there every day, developed a much closer identification with the building than did the bishop; its grandeur and glory reflected most immediately on the monastic community as worthy custodians of St Cuthbert's body. Perhaps this would not have been so much the case if other factors had not drawn the bishop apart from the cathedral, but Durham was no exception to the general trend whereby attention to affairs of state and the administration of an extensive diocese restricted a bishop's opportunities for close involvement in the life of his cathedral. Moreover bishops increasingly preferred to reside at Bishop Auckland, ten miles away, rather than in Durham Castle; experience may have taught them that close proximity tended to inflame the tensions that existed between the bishop and the cathedral community over their respective rights and privileges.

Nonetheless, in contemplation of death, the thoughts of later medieval bishops of Durham turned quite regularly to the embellishment of the cathedral. Bishop Bek (1284-1311) was the first bishop to be buried in the cathedral itself, breaching the custom of burial in the chapter-house.[14] Following this precedent a significant proportion of later bishops who held the see for a considerable period and were not translated elsewhere founded chantries in the cathedral: Thomas Hatfield (1345-81), Walter Skirlawe (1388-1406) and Thomas Langley (1406-37). Although their monuments were personal in their principal function, two also contained elements that enhanced the bishop's place in the cathedral: Hatfield provided his successors with an episcopal throne of unsurpassed loftiness over his tomb, while Langley undertook major repairs to the Galilee, where the bishop's consistory court was held alongside his tomb.

The tendency for the prior to take the lead in matters concerning the building found expression in the way that a number of priors used their personal resources to adorn the building. Prior Darlington (1258-72 and 1286-90) was credited by the monastic chronicler with the great bell-tower, presumably over the central crossing. Stonework and glass for windows was attributed to Prior Fossor (1341-74), and he had the marble and alabaster base which John Lord Neville provided for St Cuthbert's shrine brought from Newcastle after it had been shipped from London; also, together with the two monks who had prompted that project, he spurred Neville to finance the great reredos now known as the Neville screen. Prior Castell (1494-1519) renovated the great north transept window.[15]

Surviving 15th-century correspondence shows that the prior took care on occasion to keep the bishop informed about the state of the cathedral, no doubt in the hope that he might be stirred to material assistance. Thus, when the bell-tower was set on fire by lightning in 1429, Prior Wessington wrote to tell Bishop Langley of the damage to "your church"; similarly Prior Ebchester wrote to Bishop Neville in 1456 about the dilapidated state of the bell-tower of "your church", and asked for his support.[16] For all that, the prior did not feel inhibited about making appeals for help on occasion, the assumption behind his approaches was that the maintenance and repair of the building was normally the responsibility of the cathedral community, rather than the bishop. Bishop Hatfield clearly regarded the community as responsible: following a visitation he directed the monks in 1355 to make good the defects in roofing and repair of his cathedral church and its bell-tower within the space of two years.[17] When Bishop Langley made a contribution to the nave vault, the monks described it as a notable gift.[18]

It is perhaps possible to trace the community's responsibility for maintaining the cathedral right back to 1083, when Bishop William had appointed a monk as sacrist to care for the cathedral. Certainly from an early date there were funds for the maintenance of the building. By about 900 Anglo-Saxon kings had established a payment of one penny a year from each household in most regions of their kingdom for the benefit of the papacy; this was known variously as Peter's penny, hearth-penny, smoke-penny or reek-penny. Households in the diocese of Durham paid their reek-pennies not to the papacy but to the cathedral sacrist, and in 1164, when Pope Alexander III directed its enforcement for the works of St Cuthbert's church, he described this custom as ancient, perhaps suggesting that it had originated before 1083.[19] The payment of reek-pennies is recorded on later medieval accounts and rentals of the sacrist's office.[20]

Offerings from those who came to the cathedral were an important, if fluctuating, source of income. English custom was that all parishioners should visit the mother-church of their diocese every year, and they were presumably expected not to come empty-handed; in the diocese of Norwich those who failed to come were liable to pay 2s. towards the fabric, but evidence for such fines at Durham is lacking.[21] There were a number of pyxes or collecting-boxes and the accounts show that the sacrist received small sums from a number of these, but not from the most important of all, the pyx at St Cuthbert's shrine; this pyx was opened by the feretrar or shrine-keeper and his colleague, and most of the money was distributed to the individual monks, an arrangement echoing Bishop William's original intention that the collections should go towards the monks' domestic offices.[22]

A second offering of a very different kind was far less regular, but was of considerable value. When a bishop died and his body was brought to the cathedral for burial, not only did the monks keep the offerings made, together with the candles provided for the obsequies, they also claimed the chariot or hearse, the horses that drew it and their harness and caparison, and the bishop's ecclesiastical equipment, insignia, ornaments and vestments, with the bishop's seal-matrix, duly broken, being offered to St Cuthbert.[23] Vestments and ornaments could be kept and put to good use, while the silver of one seal-matrix was made into a chalice, but the hearse, the horses and their equipment were normally disposed of, for the sacrist's benefit, although it was not unknown for tight-fisted executors to attempt to frustrate the monks' claim to these.[24]

The sacrist's main source of regular income was the estate attached to his office. At Durham, as at other larger Benedictine houses, a number of separate estates supported different aspects of the monastery's life. Apart from the main estate, accounted for by the bursar, and administered by him in conjunction with the terrar, there were the estates of the almoner, the chamberlain, who provided the monks with clothing and bedding, the communar, who administered endowments given to support the celebration of anniversaries and the like, the feretrar, who was responsible for St Cuthbert's shrine, the hostiller or guest-master, the infirmarer, and the sacrist. The chief components of the sacrist's estate were land, both urban and rural, and revenues from certain parish-priests and churches in the patronage of the monastic community.

The sacrist's estate was built up in two ways. From an early date there were benefactors who gave property, not for the general support of the monks, but more specifically for the sacristy. Indeed a few made grants of wax, while others stipulated the provision of lights as the purpose for which their grants were intended. Equally, several referred to the work or fabric of the cathedral, including one in the mid-13th century, which made explicit mention of the new fabric and its support, presumably meaning the Nine Altars chapel.[25]

The second way in which the sacrist's estate grew was the result of deliberate action on the part of the monastic community itself. From the later 12 th century onwards the monks were successful in gaining permission from the pope or from their bishop for the appropriation of churches.[26] This process involved parish-churches that belonged to the monks in the sense that they had the right to put forward the priests to serve as rectors of them; appropriation meant that a church's principal revenues were permanently transferred to the monks, while a vicar, instead of a rector, served as parish-priest, with a much lower income. During the earlier 13 th century bishops became increasingly conscious that such arrangements could be detrimental to the parish involved, and consequently a strong case for appropriation had to be made. Nonetheless in 1249 Bishop Farnham allowed the monks to appropriate to the sacristy the principal revenues of the church of Bedlington in Northumberland, for the completion of the fabric of the new work and for the repair and maintenance of the roofing of the cathedral. When Bishop Kirkham (1249-60) repeated this, he was content with a more general statement of the purpose, as being for the fabric of the cathedral.[27]

During the later Middle Ages the monks were active in acquiring property, particularly in the city of Durham. While it is rarely possible to prove that this was by purchase, rather than gift, it would be remarkable if the monks had been the beneficiaries of many significant donations as late as the 14 th and 15 th centuries, and these acquisitions are surely to be seen as deliberate investments by the monastic community. Apart from the chamberlain's, every one of the monastic estates was augmented with holdings in Durham as a result; possibly this reflected the source of the funds used. So, for instance, it may have been offerings in the cathedral that enabled the community to purchase the properties whose acquisition Bishop Langley licensed in 1424 to assist with the repair of the cathedral.[28] The previous year the sacrist's estate had been improved by means of an adjustment to the main monastic estate; this involved the sacrist relinquishing to the bursar a pension from Heighington church in return for the complete lordship of Durham's Old Borough.[29]

Every monk responsible for an estate was required to present to the annual monastic chapter an account, detailing receipts and expenditures. Many of these accounts have survived; the oldest from the sacrist's office covers a period of some eighteen months, 1322-1324.[30] In medieval accounts it was normal to include entries for payments due even when nothing was received, so it is hard to use such documents for precise calculations of actual income, but it is evident that the sacrist generally received each year a sum of about £100, enough to support a small independent monastery. A major call on this was the administration of the estate, including the payment of officials and maintenance of properties; there were various other dues to be met, and also the wages of staff who assisted the sacrist in performing his functions. The sum available for the sacrist's first head of expenditure, expenses for the church, generally amounted to about a third of his income, and together with building work and repairs this had to cover the full range of altar-requisites from candles and communion-wine to vestments and plate. The regular provision available for maintaining and improving the cathedral was far from generous, and so when funds were required for new work, these had to be raised by appeals and by levying contributions from other parts of the monastery.[31]

The accounts presented by office-holders contain much information about individual monks, and give the names of those holding office; the list of sacrists from 1300 to 1539 is complete, or very nearly so.[32] During that period the office changed hands fifty-one times, giving an average term in office of rather less than five years; a few monks served more than one term. Before 1375 only two monks were in office for more than five years, but after that several served for much longer, the longest, George Cornforth, from 1481 until his death in 1507. This pattern of longer terms applied to a number of offices in the monastery during the late Middle Ages, and was perhaps a result of the decline in the size of the community, from 110 in 1300 to 66 in 1539. If the number of monks suitable for office was only just sufficient for the number of offices to be filled, there may well have been occasions when monks were kept on in office because no adequate replacement was available; another expedient is to be seen in the growing practice of one monk holding two offices simultaneously.

The information on individual sacrists makes it possible to discern how the office and its holders stood within the monastic community. Sacrists were almost invariably monks of considerable experience: those who took office between 1300 and 1539 had served as members of the community for twenty-five years on averge, suggesting an average age of about forty-five. This would have been considerably higher but for the fact that several sacrists between 1349 and 1375 had been monks for a much shorter time, one for a mere five years; this reflects the difficult circumstances after the Black Death of 1349 when fifty-two monks died, leaving only thirty-nine,[33] and it became necessary to use very recent recruits, with little experience, as office-holders. These circumstances are no doubt also the reason why this period saw the first sacrist simultaneously holding another office; that it should be as precentor strikes a rather more appropriate note than the offices held by later sacrists, who are found as terrar or principal land-agent of the community, as chancellor, responsible for the community's books and records and for the conduct of its business, or even as stock-supervisor.

From 1400 onwards sacrists tended to be rather more senior monks than before: their average length of service as monks was almost thirty years when they took office, and three had already served for more than forty years, making them about sixty years old. Somewhat before 1400 there was a return to a pattern that can be glimpsed during the 13th century when the only two Durham monks successfully elected by the community as bishops of Durham, Robert of Stichill (1260-74) and Robert of Holy Island (1274-83), had both previously served as sacrist. For most of the 14th century sacrists were not monks of such distinction; almost invariably they had already held an office involving financial administration, most commonly as almoner or hostiller, but the limit of their subsequent achievements was as head of one of the monastic dependencies or cells that belonged to Durham cathedral priory, positions of trust involving responsibility for establishments at a distance from the mother-house.

A change is marked when John of Hemingbrough became sacrist in 1363: in 1391 he was elected prior of Durham by the community. His successors, John Wessington (1416-46) and William Ebchester (1446-56), were both sacrists when they were elected as prior, and Ebchester kept the office in his hands while prior. From 1416 onwards all priors of Durham belonged to that group of monks who had been sent at an early stage in their careers to Durham College Oxford; from the late 13th century onwards the monastery had maintained a very modest number of monks at the university, but the foundation of Durham College in 1381 on Bishop Hatfield's initiative made it possible for a significant proportion of the younger monks to study there.[34] Several future sacrists were among them, and, in addition to William Ebchester, there were two, Thomas Rome and William Seton, whose academic attainments were crowned with doctorates in theology.

While it can be observed that 15th-century sacrists were not infrequently monks of greater distinction than their 14th-century predecessors, it is not so clear what this change signifies. It may simply be that a smaller community could not avoid appointing monks who would not have been burdened with such an office previously. Equally, changes in estate-management may have made it less essential for the sacrist to be an expert in administration; some late medieval sacrists of modest attainments certainly had little experience in such matters. But is it possible that the prestige of the office had grown, making it more attractive to the ambitious and gifted. Or perhaps the chance to leave some small monument exercised a stronger pull on them than it had before; at Durham, as elsewhere, it is noticeable how much emphasis was placed on building work as a measure of the achievements of late medieval ecclesiastics.[35] Quite probably there was an interplay between these various factors, but the fact that Prior Bell (1464-78) arranged for his personal *rebus* to be carved in the stonework of the new central tower indicates that there were indeed monks who were glad of the opportunity to be personally associated with the upkeep and embellishment of one of England's greatest churches.

The monastic chronicler's detailed record of the building works of bishops and priors demonstrates the value placed on such works by the community. In some cases these works contributed directly to its comfort and convenience, but others brought less material benefits. Quite how these benefits may be rightly defined is less certain, for few medieval writers provide any insight into the impact upon them of the works of human hands. There was among the 12th-century monks of Durham one outstanding exception, Prior Lawrence (c.1149-54). His verse dialogues are famed for their description of Durham, for their celebration of the way in which art enhanced the city's natural advantages. Yet Lawrence disappoints: the art of which he wrote was much more a matter of ingenuity than creativity, and his enhancements were not objects of beauty but strong fortifications capable of resisting attacks by the Scots. When he wrote of the cathedral his concern was to deplore the profanities committed in it by invading soldiers.[36] Had be been asked about its aesthetic impact upon him, the question might well have puzzled him.

Almost four centuries of monks followed Prior Lawrence, and it may be correct to suppose that late in the Middle Ages there were individual monks who derived personal aesthetic satisfaction from the beauties of the building in which they worshipped every day. The famous late 16th-century reminiscences of "the monasticall church of Durham before the suppression", the *Rites of Durham*, gives descriptions of the building and its contents that seem to be replete with epithets of aesthetic appreciation, such as "sumptuouslie finished", "curiously wrought", "fynly adorned", "most artificiallie and cunyngly compiled and framed". Yet it is far from clear, even with an object described as "a goodly sighte for all the beholders", that what prompted admiration was the beauty of the object itself, rather than the conspicuous lavishness of its materials and workmanship.[37]

Sumptuousness and size were qualities that certainly counted for much in the Middle Ages,[38] both for great lords and their households and for cathedrals. Such qualities demonstrated a capacity to sustain the dignity and honour of an established place in the order of things. Late in the 11th century the bishop and his new cathedral community set about showing their capacity as custodians of the relics of St Cuthbert by undertaking the construction of a striking new building, and the saint's seal of approval was made plain in 1104 when his remains were found to be still incorrupt. In practice it was the monastic community that came to bear the principal responsibility for the cult of Saint Cuthbert,[39] and an essential element of this involved ensuring that his great church was as fine as possible. If this were not done, the monks' failure to uphold the saint's dignity would be reflected in a withdrawal of his favour. No bishop could countenance this, particularly when Scottish incursions could serve so readily as manifestations of St Cuthbert's displeasure, and the community's reputation would have been seriously damaged if the people of the region had been able to blame their sufferings on the dishonour done to their tutelary saint through the negligence of the monks.

The cult of St Cuthbert was central to the monastic community's sense of its own particular purpose, and the destruction of his shrine apparently shattered all resistance at Durham to the suppression of religious houses under King Henry VIII. The despoliation of the shrine and its relics, described in poignant detail in the *Rites of Durham*, seems to have taken place late in December 1539; on the last day of that month the community surrendered to the king.[40]

In a sense all was not lost, for the old forms of worship were not superseded immediately, and indeed continued well after the law prescribed otherwise; nor was there a wholesale campaign for removing from the building all features that might be characterized as popish or idolatrous.[41] What was quite quickly lost was the cathedral chapter's settled unanimity of view on the function of the building. The Anglican establishment came to encompass very considerable diversity of individual religious opinion, and this diversity was commonly reflected among the canons who formed the reformed chapter. At times one party might find itself in the ascendant, and able to bring in changes,[42] but enthusiasm must have been dampened by an awareness that partisan policies might soon be reversed, while a sense of commitment to the building was hardly fostered by the fact that canons were free to reside away from Durham for most of their time. In general, therefore, the chapter often pursued a relatively inactive *via media*, adopting compromises that were not close to any individual canon's heart. Little surprise then that there was rarely much sign of that ardour for embellishing the building which had imbued the monastic community. Over the centuries since 1539 little has been added to the building and in happy consequence the magnificance of the medieval work can be enjoyed without hindrance.

8 The Cathedral and its Early Books

Roger Norris

The Library of the Dean and Chapter of Durham - the library of the cathedral - contains the largest number of volumes *in situ* for any monastic house in this country. About 600 volumes (of which 80 are printed books) survive from the mediaeval Durham Priory in libraries throughout Great Britain.[1] Of these, over 350 remain in their home, Durham Cathedral. Detailed catalogues or inventories date from the third quarter of the 12th century, from 1391, 1395 and 1416, together with smaller lists, which indicate that at this early time there were some 900 volumes. No catalogue survives that takes us into the realm of the printed book, though it is clear from the annotations on some early printed books that the monks continued to acquire. Greenslade sets out the great spread of learning encompassed in the Cathedral, though he says it was not a storehouse of rare texts, and suggests that by the time of the Dissolution, with only two texts in Greek and "scarcely a breath of the Renaissance", the monks may have been an intellectual backwater.[2] He is, nonetheless, at pains to indicate that all the criteria were met for Durham to be regarded as a nucleus of learned if not innovative brethren. Scholarly texts were integral to the monastic life at Durham Priory, at the associated cells and at Durham College, Oxford.

Rites of Durham, written in 1593, reminds us that in the days of the Priory the north alley of Durham Cathedral cloister contained

> "great almeries (cupboards) of waynscott all full of bookes ... so that every one dyd studye what Docter (of the Church) pleased them best, havinge the librarie at all tymes to goe studie in besydes there (their) Carrells", and that in the angle on the south side of the dormitory door "ther is a stronghowse called ye treasure howse ... and in the midst of itt was a great (grate) of iron from ye ground to ye roofe".[3]

This treasurehouse is more familiarly known now and likewise in the 14th and 15th centuries as the Spendement or Splendement, a term uniquely applied to this room at Durham. The term features in all the mediaeval book catalogues except that of the 12th century, and late mediaeval hands marked the first leaf of many volumes as being located in the Spendement. It is still an imposing room with the grill dividing the west section from the east. Piper identifies that a new library room was constructed mainly under John Wessington (prior 1416-46) between 1414 and 1418 in the area now used as the Song School in the east cloister next to the Chapter House.[4] Books for this room came both from the cloister cupboards and the Spendement, probably numbering originally about 150 and growing to 300.The books placed in this new 'Librarie' can be identified by their distinctive library location marks indicating the bookcase, the shelf and the place of each thereon.

The collection at Durham now contains specially important books of Saxon, 11th and 12th century dates. These were splendidly catalogued in the 1930s by Sir Roger Mynors, and it is his work that scholars continue to use as a base for their studies.[5] We will consider them according to two broad time periods.

Saxon Beginning

A core of those books which predate the eventual establishment of the shrine of St.

Cuthbert at Durham come from the Saxon scriptorium of the double monastery of Wearmouth-Jarrow, a major centre of learning and art under the abbots Benedict Biscop and Ceolfrid in the 7th century, and home of the Venerable Bede. Egfrith, king of Northumbria, had given Biscop 70 hides of land to found a monastery at Wearmouth. Biscop visited continental Europe five times, energetically fostering the cross-fertilisation of cultures and brining back ideas, artifacts and manuscripts, including books from the Italian monastery at Vivarium, founded by Cassiodorus Senator. An 8th century copy of Cassiodorus's *Commentary on the Psalms* (Ms.B.II.30) is one of the most splendid reminders of this period which is still at Durham. The great codex contains two full-page illustrations of David, one of him as a psalmist, seated within the frame of a chair, holding a harp, the whole surrounded by eighteen compartments of interlace work, some inhabited by lively beasts or birds. The second, in a fine state of preservation has David as warrior. The bold lines of his figure, bisected from lower-left to upper-right by his spear and the ten intricate interlace panels which provide a frame, indicate the strong artistic sense of form and layout of the Saxon illustrator. That none of it is haphazard has been established by George and Iain Bain, father and son, in their analyses of the geometric make up of such pages.[6]

The *Lindisfarne Gospels*, written and probably decorated by Eadfrith (Bishop of Lindisfarne 698-74) as a tribute to St Cuthbert, is the finest example of Northumbrian work. It is now in the British Library as Ms. Cotton Nero D.iv.[7] It is however recorded under the title *Evangelia* in an inventory of 1367 as still belonging to Durham Priory. The British Library kindly allowed this book to be in Durham on the occasion in 1987 of the thirteen hundredth anniversary of the death of St Cuthbert. Opportunity was taken to lay it at the Saint's shrine, a poignant reminder of the greatness of Anglo-Saxon culture and faith.

There remains in perfect condition one book of this early date which was intimately associated with St Cuthbert. It is known as the Stonyhurst Gospel through the home of its owners, The Community of the Society of Jesus, in whose care it has been since 1769.[8] A copy of St John's Gospel, it was probably written in the last years of the 7th century at Wearmouth-Jarrow. In a clear, beautiful hand, called technically capitular insular, its dimensions measure only 5½ inches by 3½ inches. The 94 original leaves of the volume are encased in its original binding. Bindings have ever been commonly subject to damage or ill-advised repair or replacement. Yet this book, bound in deep-red goatskin, still has the modelled and incised decoration on the front-board and incised decoration on the back, of a quality comparable with the best in Northumbrian manuscript decoration. Yellow inlay survives widely on the front, with a satchel of red leather, instead of clasps, to keep the vellum book closed. This volume is the book seen by Durham monks lying at the head on the board of the saint's coffin at the Translation of St Cuthbert's body to the present feretory in 1104, and which Bishop Flambard displayed to the congregation as a miracle of preservation at that time. The Stonyhurst Gospel was also brought back to Durham for a short time in 1987.

Contemporary with the Stonyhurst Gospel and at home in Durham is Ms.A.11.17, a fragmentary Gospel book, one text of the early 8th century and a smaller fragment of the late 7th.[9] The book was rebound as an example of his best work by Roger Powell in 1976. The first folio shows a full page decoration of the opening words of St John's Gospel "In principio erat verbum" - "In the beginning was the Word". Although much worn, this is a magnificent page in the tradition of the *Lindisfarne Gospels*, the first three letters INP coalescing in a multitude of framed long-necked and long-beaked birds, and there at the top right-hand, in a late mediaeval hand, the location : de le splendement. The book has been broken up at various stages, probably being reassembled in the 17th century, and the majestic Christ in Glory Crucified illumination on folio 38v has clearly been dissociated and used separately, perhaps as an object of special reverence.

The seven dispersed leaves of a gospel book in Mss. A.II.10, C.III.13, and C.III.20, provide Durham's earliest example of 7th century insular decoration with a monogram INI for the start of the word Initium at the beginning of St. Mark on f.2R and, on f.3v, a leaf originally preceding and containing a framework of three "D"-like loops one above the other. The lower two are filled with the Greek text of the Lord's Prayer in Latin characters. The individual plaited decoration of the loops is intricate and mathematically perfect.

It is apparent that such books, which we now regard with the respect as forceful examples of art, learning and history, were neglected in the late Middle Ages. They were sometimes broken up and cut down to provide fly leaves and protection for books written at a much later date. To some extent, doubtless, survival was accidental in a monastic house which had a workmanlike and thorough approach to the virtues of academic learning.

From the sojourn of the St. Cuthbert Community at Chester-le-Street (883-995) stems a Wessex book, *The Lives of St Cuthbert* by the Venerable Bede, a gift of King Athelstan in 934. (This is now at Corpus Christi College, Cambridge, Ms. 183). Its frontispiece, of the king offering a book to St Cuthbert, is possibly the earliest presentation picture in English art. During the Chester-le-Street period Aldred, designated provost of the Community, made a translation of the Gospels into Anglo-Saxon and wrote this in a distinctive hand in red ink between the lines of the late-7th century *Lindisfarne Gospels*, providing a literary and historical enhancement to a book profoundly associated with the spirituality of the Cuthbert tradition.

A small book of the eighth decade of the 10th century, Durham's Ms. A.IV.19, similarly has an Anglo-Saxon interlinear gloss by Aldred, done for Aelfsige, bishop of Chester-le-Street.[10] It is often the case that it is the small books which have suffered the roughest treatment. The larger more splendid books, from their beauty and size, are more likely to survive. Ms. A.IV.19 has had heavy usage and is in a poor modern binding. It is essentially a liturgical compilation of collects and short chapters to be used by the Community for their daily offices. At the end of the book are four collects for the intercession of St. Cuthbert. The characteristic red-ink additons of Aldred provide a humble link with the great *Lindisfarne Gospels*.

The Benedictine Collection

Books such as those mentioned above provided the nucleus for a library when the Community arrived at Durham in 995, to grow into one of the great monastic collections. The Community of St. Cuthbert was translated into a community of monks organised after the rule of St. Benedict in 1083 by Bishop William of St. Calais. The new Benedictine Community was built substantially on the personel of the revived foundation of Jarrow and Wearmouth, 23 monks, and Bishop William provide them with a large group of about 50 books, the names of which are recorded on the fly-leaf of the second and last volume of a magnificent Bible, Durham Ms. A.II.4. Of the original volumes, about 20 are still at Durham, and it is a matter of discussion whether these are English or French books.

The books of William of St Calais at Durham represent a high point in manuscript writing and decoration. The vellum is white and supple - in contrast to the early Saxon books which often have thick and translucent pages. The hands are clear and full of character, the colour varying between dark and light browns. The decoration is a riot of the imaginative, in pastel shades of red, blue, yellow and green, the initials inhabited with foliage, lions, heads, persons struggling to emerge, in a fretwork of interlace ribbon. Scalloped ornament and fine outline are typical of the work. The figures have eccentricity analogous with contemporary architectural sculpture such as is visible within the north and south doors of Durham Cathedral.

Outstanding in Bishop William's books are Mss A.II.4, B.II.13 and B.II.22. The first mentioned, containing the latter part of the Old Testament and the complete New Testament, originally had a first companion volume, now lost. Special is the introductory initial, f.65R, to the Psalms, the B of "Beatus vir ..." psalm 1, "Happy is the man". This is often used as the occasion for extravagant decoration in mediaeval work, and here shows David as a psalmist, harp in hand, inhabiting the lower part of the letter. In the upper part is a dog-like creature, and beaked heads guard the head and tail of the left support. This is a massive book, 19.5 x 12.3 inches.

Ms. B.II.13, the second of three volumes of commentary on the Psalms, has on folio 102R as an introduction to Psalm 60 a tripartite initial I with Christ at the head, a full length depiction of Bishop William in the centre in a green chasuble and holding a crosier, and, at the foot, the kneeling figure of Robert Benjamin the illuminator. Surrounding all is a prayer for the bishop and for his servant Robert. There is no reason to consider the two portraits of William and Robert as other than from true life (Fig. 72).

The 11th and 12th centuries were the great ages of Durham's manuscripts, presenting so many facets of interest. Ms. Hunter 100, an early 12th century composition of astrological, medical and mathematical works, from the collection of the 17/18th century Durham physician and antiquarian Christopher Hunter, provides delightful zodiacal figures and surgical illustrations. The artistry in the book is similar in style to another Durham book dated c.1100-1120 now at Oxford (University College Ms.165), Bede's *Life of St Cuthbert*, with its more than 50 narrative illustrations. It is the earliest illustrated *Life*. From the later 12th century is Ms.A.IV.35. It is a collection of the lives of Saints Cuthbert, Aidan and Oswald, a fine small book in itself, but with the additional fore-edge paintings of the three saints, one on each edge.

A book which escaped the good offices of the 19th century rebinder of many of Durham's mediaeval books is the early 12th century Ms.A.IV.34, a commentary on the Song of Songs. These 68 folios have never been bound, a condition which must have been widespread at the time of its writing when such books were described as "in uno quaterno" - wrapped in another piece of vellum. The survival of this form provides the scholar with many clues as to the make-up of a book - the folding of the vellum and the ruling of the page. Most books were ruled blind, with a blunt instrument, until the end of the 11th century.

The portrait of the author Augustine, in an 11th century De Civitate Dei (another St Calais Ms.B.II.22) is an outstanding piece and of a different character and delicacy from others in the group. The initial G, itself a design of almost Renaissance flamboyance with animals intertwining, contains Augustine himself seated at a tripod desk. In one hand is his goosequill pen in the other his knife - used for sharpening and repairing the pen and also to restrain the

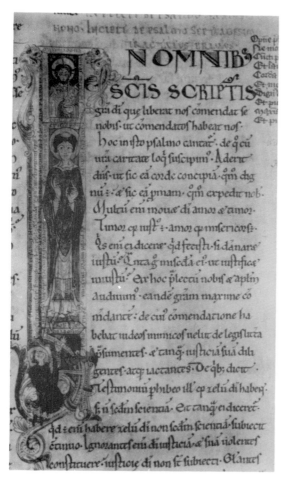

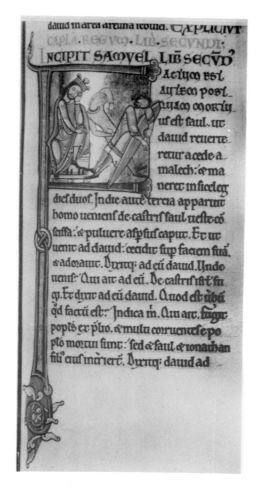

Fig. 72 William of St. Calais, Ms B II 13, 11th century commentary on psalms

Fig. 73 **Hugh of le Puiset, Ms B II 13, 12th century, David mourning over Saul and Jonathan**

springy vellum on which he writes. Depictions of the art of writing are not uncommon in mediaeval art; another is in the lower left-hand corner of the first folio, uncoloured Christ in Majesty of Ms.A.IV.10 - a glossed Matthew of the collection of Hugh of Le Puiset - where the evangelical figure for Mark, a lion, is similarly shown.

Gullick has closely analysed the St Calais group of manuscripts at Durham, relating them to contemporary survivals in other libraries and postulating that at least nine are of French, possibly Bayeaux, origin.[11] He indentifies three artists by name - William in Ms.B.II.14, Robert Benjamin in Ms.B.II.13, and Hugo Pictor in Ms.B.II.19 - and distinguishes the various unnamed scribes of the books. His purpose is to confirm the variety of sources, and that books were not even then necessarily written by monks. Gullick's hypothesis is re-inforced by Parkes's analysis of Ms.B.II.22.[12]

The great building bishop, Hugh of Le Puiset (1153-1195), again of French origin, gave over 70 books to Durham monastery, a benefaction of similar importance to that of St Calais. The magnificence of his secular achievements as well as his ecclesiastical prestige is reflected in the grandeur and forceful artistry of some of the 13 surviving books which can be identified as emanating from his benefaction, some of them containing the library inscription "Hugonis episcopi" : the book of Hugh the bishop.

The manuscripts of Le Puiset are distinguished by the strength of the hands with their dark black ink - thick and viscous, composed of galls, gum and copperas - which contrasts with the lighter brown of varying shades of the 11th century St Calais books. The St Calais hands are graceful, whilst those of the Le Puiset books are hard and Gothic, more, as it were, what one might expect to see generally in mediaeval books. The decorated illustrations of Le Puiset's benefection are stylised, more sophisticated and purposeful than those of St. Calais, and the colours are deeper and seemingly more sure (Fig. 73).

The five outstanding books of Le Puiset are Mss.A.II.19 and A/II/1, vols. 1-4. The Epistles of St Paul with the Commentary of Peter Lombard (A.II.19) is a huge book of over 300 folios, and at the head of each Epistle is an introductory initial P with figures and animals, some of the initials having a piece of linen sewn above to protect their beauty. The gold used on these letters and in other Le Puiset books, set on a cushion of albumen (egg-white), has an immediate freshness. The vellum, in contrast to the thick and horny vellum of the Anglo-Saxon books, is soft and white.

The four-volume Bible (Ms.A.II.1), Le Puiset's greatest manuscript legacy, has unfortunately been vandalised. There is no proof that the nursemaid of the children of Prebendary Henry Dobson (6th stall 1695-1718) cut out some of the glorious intitials to divert her charges, but that is the story. (Fully authenticated is the gift by the Dean and Chapter of a slip of the 8th century Gospel book (Ms.A.II.16) to Samuel Pepys for his palaeographical collection; the slip is now in the Pepysian Library at Magdalene College, Cambridge). Le Puiset's Ms.A.II.1, nonetheless, still has many great decorated initials remaining, including in volume 3 the outstanding I at the beginning of the Book of Esther showing the head of King Ahasuerus, the figure of Esther and below that of Haman hanging from the gallows, and the famous E at the beginning of I Maccabees where the troops of Alexander of Macedon are in conflict with those of Darius of Persia, all in the battledress of the 12th century. In Volume 4 the Canon Tables, which provide a tabulated comparison of the four Gospel books, are designed as arcades reminiscent of the arcading of the wall-aisles of Durham Cathedral.

Each volume of this set has some relaid fragments of the original blind-stamped (i.e. uncoloured) 12th century binding on the 19th century rebinding. Five metal bosses, probably of a much later date though with mediaeval precedent, front and back on each book, protect the bindings from harm on any surface. These 12th century decorated bindings have designs of an invention and fluency lost in the roll-stamped bindings of the later Middle Ages.[13]

The Library does contain two relatively unspoilt plain white pigskin bindings of the 12th century, Mss.A.IV.11 and A.IV.13. In both it is possible to see the careful construction of the bindings with sewings and the raised-band extensions into the leather-covered wood of the binding intact. In the first the embroidered head and tail leather spine-flaps are also present. Vellum is a lively material, reacting quickly to the environment, and the larger the book the more solid and heavy the binding, to protect the text, to hold the gatherings of the vellum folios together, and, with the assistance of clasps, to keep the pages flat.

Concluding Comments

A great loss, in common with most monastic houses, is the quantity of liturgical **books** which must have abounded in the Priory. The psalters and service-books, personal to each brother and perhaps handed down one to another, are gone, probably immediately at the Dissolution of the Monastery 1539/40. Also lost are the more secular of the texts in the library, the classics especially such as Ovid, Juvenal, Virgil and Terence, which are mentioned in the mediaeval catalogues and which provided light reading. There is still a good 12th century Suetonius, *Lives of the Twelve Caesars* (Ms.C.III.18), but otherwise only a selection of the more sober Latin classics, Cicero, Priscian and Prudentius, survive.

The catholic nature of the mediaeval collection is nonetheless fully represented at Durham still. Some of the better-known names are the texts of the *Chronicles of Symeon of Durham*, a 12th-century copy of the *Ecclesiastical History of the English Nation* by the Venerable Bede, Laurence of Durham's *Hypognosticon,* Reginald of Durham on the *Miracles of St Cuthbert*, two French verse epics by Gaimar and Wace with an anonymous *Romance of Alexander the Great*, Latin translations of Aristotle, works of theology by Augustine, Aquinas, Gregory, Chrysostom, Anselm and Bernard, and the standard late-mediaeval law books, often brought in from the stationers' companies of Italy, of Gratian and Justinian.

In the present century through the generosity of the Friends of Durham Cathedral and other organisations and individuals, it is occasionally possible to bring back Durham mediaeval books that come on the market. For instance, in the last 30 years a 13/14th century Bible from the Durham cell of Stamford (Ms.C.III.23) and a fragmentary series of Benedictine precepts and dispensations from the early 15th century (Ms.B.IV.49) have found a lasting home in the Spendement.

The Durham Dean and Chapter Library today is a working library, frequented by students of all sorts of experience and from international locations, although for the sake of preservation, care has to be taken that, with the growth in interest and minuteness of modern historical scholarship, Saxon and Mediaeval books are not used more in a few decades of the 20th century than they have been in the many previous centuries of their history. Nevertheless, the Durham Benedictine tradition of providing a welcome to scholars and scholarship is in good heart.

Bishops of Durham

955-1018	Aldhun	1530-59	Cuthbert Tunstall
1020-41	Eadmund	1561-76	James Pilkington
1041-??	Eadred	1577-87	Richard Barnes
1042-56	Aethelric	1589-95	Matthew Hutton
1056-71	Aethelwin	1595-1606	Tobias Matthew
1071-80	Walcher	1606-17	William James
1081-96	William of St. Calais	1617-27	Richard Neile
1099-1128	Rannulph Flambard	1628	George Monteigne
1133-40	Geoffrey Rufus	1628-32	John Howson
1143-52	William of St. Barbara	1632-59	Thomas Morton
1153-95	Hugh of Le Puiset	1660-72	John Cosin
1197-1208	Philip of Poitou	1674-1722	Nathaniel Crewe
1217-26	Richard Marsh	1722-30	William Talbot
1229-37	Richard le Poor	1730-50	Edward Chandler
1241-48	Nicolas Farnham	1750-52	Joseph Butler
1249-60	Walter Kirkham	1752-71	Richard Trevor
1260-74	Robert Stichill	1771-87	John Egerton
1274-83	Robert of Holy Island	1787-91	Thomas Thurlow
1284-1310	Antony Bek	1791-1826	The Hon. Shute Barrington
1311-16	Richard Kellaw	1826-36	William Van Mildert
1318-33	Lewis de Beaumont	1836-56	Edward Maltby
1333-45	Richard of Bury	1856-60	Charles Thomas Longley
1345-81	Thomas Hatfield	1860-1	The Hon. Henry Montague Villiers
1382-88	John Fordham	1861-78	Charles Baring
1388-1406	Walter Skirlaw	1879-89	Joseph Barber Lightfoot
1406-37	Thomas Langley	1889-1901	Brooke Foss Westcott
1437-57	Robert Neville	1901-20	Handley Carr Glyn Moule
1457-76	Laurence Booth	1920-39	Herbert Hensley Henson
1476-83	William Dudley	1939-52	Alwyn Terrel Petre Williams
1484-94	John Sherwood	1952-56	Arthur Michael Ramsey
1994-1501	Richard Fox	1956-66	Maurice Henry Harland
1502-05	William Senhouse	1966-72	Ian Thomas Ramsey
1507-8	Christopher Bainbridge	1973-83	John Stapylton Habgood
1509-23	Thomas Ruthall	1984-94	David Edward Jenkins
1523-29	Thomas Wolsey	1994-	Michael Turnbull

Priors and Deans of Durham

Priors		Deans	
1083-87	Aldwin	1541-48	Hugh Whitehead
1087-1109	Turgot	1551-53	Robert Horne
1109-37	Algar	1553-57	Thomas Watson
1137-49	Roger	1557-59	Thomas Robertson
1149-53	Lawrence	1559-60	Robert Horne
1154-58	Absolom	1560-63	Ralph Skinner
1158-62	Thomas	1563-79	William Whittingham
1163-86	German	1580-81	Thomas Wilson (lay)
1188-1208	Bertram	1583-95	Tobias Matthew
1209-14	William	1596-1606	William James
1214-33	Ralph Kermet	1606-20	Sir Adam Newton (lay)
1233-44	Thomas of Melsonby	1620-38	Richard Hunt
1244-58	Bertram of Middleton	1639-45	Walter Balcanquall
1258-72	Hugh of Darlington	1645-59	William Fuller
1272-85	Richard of Claxton	1660-61	John Barwick
1285-89	Hugh of Darlington	1662-84	John Sudbury
1289-1308	Richard of Hoton	1684-91	Dennis Granville
1308-13	William of Tanfield	1691-99	Thomas Comber
1314-22	Geoffrey of Burdon	1690-1728	John Montague
1322-41	William of Cowton	1728-46	Henry Bland
1341-74	John Fossor	1746-74	Spencer Cowper
1374-91	Robert of Berrington	1774-77	Thomas Dampier
1391-1416	John of Hemmingburgh	1777-88	William Digby
1416-46	John of Washington	1788-94	John Hinchcliff (bishop)
1446-56	William of Ebchester	1794-1824	James, Earl Cornwallis (bishop)
1456-64	John Burnaby	1824-27	Charles Henry Hall
1464-78	Richard Bell	1827-40	John Banks Jenkinson (bishop)
1478-84	Robert of Ebchester	1840-69	George Waddington
1484-94	John of Auckland	1869-94	William Charles Lake
1494-1519	Thomas Castell	1894-1912	George William Kitchin
1524-40	Hugh Whitehead	1912-18	Herbert Hensley Henson
		1918-33	James Edward Cowell Welldon
		1933-51	Cyril Argentine Alington
		1951-73	John Herbert Severn Wild
		1974-79	Eric William Heaton
		1980-88	Peter Richard Baelz
		1989-	John Robert Arnold

References

Chapter 1

1. G. Bonner, D.W. Rollason, C. Stancliffe (eds) *St. Cuthbert, His Cult and Community to A.D. 1200*, Boydell Press: Woodbridge (1989).
2. A. Thacker, 'Lindisfarne and the origins of the cult of St. Cuthbert', in G. Bonner et al., *op. cit.*, 103-22.
3. B. Colgrave (ed., trans) *Two Lives of Cuthbert*, Cambridge, C.U.P. (1985).
4. L. Sherley-Price (trans) *Bede: A History of the English Church and People*, Penguin, Harmondsworth (1982).
5. D. Rollason, *Saints and Relics in Anglo-Saxon England*, Basil Blackwell: Oxford (1989).
6. D.W. Rollason (ed), *Cuthbert, Saint and Patron*, Dean & Chapter: Durham (1987).
7. B. Colgrave, 'St. Cuthbert and his times', in C.F. Battiscombe (ed), *The Relics of St. Cuthbert*, O.U.P: Oxford (1956), 115-43.
8. W.M. Aird, 'St. Cuthbert, the Scots and the Normans', in M. Chibnall (ed) *Anglo-Norman Studies XVI: Proceedings of the Battle Conference, 1993*, Boydell Press: Woodbridge (1994), 1-20.
9. Simeon of Durham (trans. Joseph Stephenson) *A History of the Church of Durham*, Llanerc Enterprises, facsimile reprint: Lampeter (1988).
10. D. Pocock (ed), *Visions of Durham*, City of Durham Trust: Durham (1990).
11. N. Pevsner, *Outline of European Architecture*, Penguin: Harmondsworth (1963), 66.
12. G. Zarnecki, J. Holt, T. Holland (eds), *English Romanesque Art, 1066-1200*, G. Weidenfeld & Nicholson,Ltd: London (1984).
13. T.G. Jackson, *Byzantine and Romanesque Architecture*, C.U.P: Cambridge (1913), vol. 2, 233.
14. D. Pocock, and R. Gazzard, *Durham: Portrait of a Cathedral City*, City of Durham Trust and Department of Geography: Durham (1983), 25-43.

Chapter 2

1. This opinion is challenged by David McGee, "The 'early vaults' of St-Etienne at Beauvais", *Journal of the Society of Architectural Historians*, XLV (1984), 20-31.
2. For a review of the literature on this point and a convincing alternative interpretation of the quadrant arches, see S. Gardner, "The nave galleries of Durham Cathedral", *Art Bulletin*, LXIV (1982), 564-79.
3. For a convenient summary, see M.G. Snape, "Documentary evidence for the building of Durham Cathedral and its monastic buildings", *Medieval Art and Architecture of Durham Cathedral, British Archaelogical Conference Transactions for 1977* (1980) 20-36.
4. K.W. Markuson, "Recent investigation in the east range of the cathedral monastery, Durham", *Medieval Art and Architecture* (1980) *op.cit.*, 37-48.
5. W.H. St John Hope, "Recent discoveries in the cloister of Durham Abbey", *Archaeologia*, LVIII (1903), 1-24.
6. T. Arnold (ed), *Symeonis Monachi Opera Omnia*, Rolls Series, 75 (1882), 128-29.
7. J. Bilson, "The east end of Durham Cathedral", *Journal of the Royal Institute of British Architects*, 11 (1896) 546-48; J. Bilson, "Recent discoveries at the east end of Durham Cathedral", *Archaeological Journal*, LIII (1896) 1-18.
8. E. Fernie, "The effect of the Conquest on Norman architectural patronage", *Anglo-Norman Studies*, IX (1986), 71-85.
9. P. Frankl, *The Gothic: Literary Sources and Interpretations through Eight Centuries*, Princeton (1960), 763-72, 798-826.
10. R. Mark, *Experiments in Gothic Structure*, Cambridge, Mass., 1982, 102-117.
11. J. James, "The rib vaults of Durham Cathedral", *Gesta*, XXII (1983), 139-140.
12. J. Bilson, "Durham Cathedral: the chronology of its vaults", *Archaeological Journal*, LXXIX (1922), 156.
13. J. Bony, "Durham et la tradition saxonue", *Etudes d'Art Medievale Offertes a Louis Grodecki*, Paris (1981), 79-85.
14. E. Fernie, "The spiral piers of Durham Cathedral", *Medieval Art and Architecture* (1980) *op.cit.*, 51-56.
15. J. Bilson (1922), *op.cit.*, 123-128.
16. *Ibid.*, 123-124.
17. The latter scheme is reconstructed by J. James, "The rib vaults of Durham Cathedral", *Gesta* XXII (1983), 135-45.

18. I. Curry, "Aspects of the Anglo-Norman design of Durham Cathedral", *Archaeologia Aeliana*, 5th Series, XIV (1986) 45, fig.8.

19. In 1072 Earl Waltheof commerced the castle "where the bishop could enclose himself with his men out of danger from invaders". Bishop Flambard built a curtain wall from the east end of the cathedral up to the castle and levelled the space between them. - W.Page (ed) *Victoria History of the Counties of England: Durham*, vol. III, London (1928) 64-93.

20. Bony argues that transept high vaults were not part of the initial plan. - "Le project premier de Durham: voutement partiel ou voutement total?" in *Urbanisme et Architecture Etudes ecrites et publices en l'honneur de Pierre Lavedan*, Paris (1954), 41-49. Bilson (1922), *op.cit.*, suggests they were.

21. On the Anglo-Saxon cathedral see E. Cambridge in H.D. Briggs, E. Cambridge and R.N. Bailey, "A new approach to church archaeology: dowsing, excavation and documentary work at Woodhorn, Ponteland and the pre-Norman cathedral at Durham", *Archaeologia Aeliana*, Series 5, XI (1983), 91-97.

22. J.P. McAleer, "Romanesque England and the development of the Facade Harmonique", *Gesta*, XXIII/2 (1984), 87-105.

23. J. Bony, "The stonework planning of the first Durham Master" in E. Firnie and P. Crossley (eds) *Medieval Architecture and its Intellectual Context: Studies in Honour of Peter Kidson*, London (1990), 19-34.

24. T.S.R. Boase, *English Art, 1100-1216*, Oxford (1953), 21; K. Galbraith (unpublished), "Notes on sculpture in Durham", London, Society of Antiquities, MS 903/6/1,3 suggests an Islamic source from Spain, such as Toledo, Cristo de la Luz, for the intersecting arcades at Durham. She also allies the rib-vaults and chevron with this course (MS 903/6/12, p.7).

25. For a detailed account of the chapel, see R. Halsey, "The Galilee Chapel", *Medieval Art and Architecture* (1980) *op.cit.*, 59-73.

26. For a detailed account of the schapel, see P. Draper, "The Nine Altars at Durham and Fountains", *ibid.*, 74-86.

27. G. Russell, "The North Window of the Nine Altars Chapel, Durham Cathedral", *ibid.*, 87-89.

28. *Royal Commission on Ancient and Historical Monuments of Scotland: Fife, Kinross and Clackmannan* (1933), 106-111: fig.226.

29. E. Cambridge, "The architectural context of the Romanesque cathedral at Kirkwell, in B.E. Crawford (ed), *St. Magnus Cathedral and Orkney's 12th Century Renaissance*, Aberdeen (1988), 111-126.

30. E. Cambridge, "The early building-history of St. Andrew's Cathedral, Fife, and its context in northern Transitional architecture", *Antiquaries Journal* 57 (1977), 277-288.

31. C.H. Moore, "The aisle vaulting of Winchester transcept", *Journal of Royal Institute of British Architects*, XXIII (1916), 313-20, 329-34.

32. Y.M. Froidevaux, "L'abbatiale de Lessay", *Les monuments historiques de la France*, 4 (1958), 139-140.

33. W.W. Clark, "The nave of Saint-Pierre at Lisieux: Romanesque structure in a Gothic guise", *Gesta* XVI/I (1977), 29-38.

34. The importance of the decorative aspect of Romanesque Durham was emphasised by G. Webb, *Architecture in Britain: the Middle Ages*, Penguin: Harmondsworth (1956), 38-39; see also T.S.R. Boase (1953) *op.cit.*, 21; P. Kidson, P. Murray and P. Thompson, *A History of English Architecture*, Penguin: Harmondsworth (1979), 53; J. Bony (1981) *op.cit.*, 79-80. Bilson (1899) op.cit. 289-319, sees the complex arch mouldings as forerunners of English Gothic mouldings.

Chapter 3

Shortened Titles Used.
ACM - *Abstracts of Chapter Minutes*. Vol.I to 1726, Vol.II 1726 to 1829, Vol.III 1829 to 1867. Dean and Chapter Library, Durham.
Record - Record of Works done in and upon the Cathedral Church of Durham 1700 to 1857 and 1858 to 1864. Privately printed. Dean and Chapter Library.

1. John Harvey, *English Mediaeval Architects* (1984), 345. R. Wolveston is described as "vir artificiosus fuisset opere et prudens architectus in omni structura artis forisseae" by Reginald of Durham.

2. Martin G. Snape, *Medieval Art and Architecture*, op.cit., 28-29.

3. *ACM* Vol.I 18 Aug. 1631.

4. *ACM* Vol.I 3 Nov. 1660. Prior to this meeting there had been no Chapter Minutes since 2 Dec. 1642.

5. *ACM* Vol.I 6 Nov. 1660. Letter had been received from the King giving instructions on the collection of certain rents to help with repairs to the church fabric. The Chapter was also concerned to check on timber in the Chapter woods for the repairs.
6. N. Pevsner (revised E. Willaimson), *op.cit.*, 119.
7. *ACM* 5 Oct. 1661 Page 185-6. George Dallam was of the prominent family of organ builders. Thomas Dallam had built an organ for Dean Hunt in 1620. George Dallam's new organ cost £550. and was in use by the end of 1662.
8. Conrad Eden, *Organs of Durham Cathedral* (1970), 6-7. Bernard Smith was in competition with the equally distinguished Renatus Harris for building the Durham organ. Harris had built the Newcastle St. Nicholas organ, and gave a lower estimate, but Smith was awarded the contract.
9. *ACM* 2 June 1720 and 20 Nov. 1720.
10. *ACM*, 582.
11. *ACM* Page 582. The report is included in the Dean and Chapter Additional MSS.
12. W. Hutchinson, *History of Durham* (1787), first edition with plates, vol. 2, 227.
13. *ACM*, 629.
14. *ACM*, 634. 20 Nov. 1795.
15. Billings mentions the colossal heads of the founders, William Carilef and Rufus - R.W. Billings, *Architectural Illustrations and Description of the Cathedral church at Durham*, London (1843), 14.
16. William Greenwell, *Durham Cathedral* (1881), 8th edition, 1913, 33.
17. *ACM* 20 Nov. 1804. 668.
18. Dean & Chapter Additional MSS.
19. *ACM* 21 July 1806.
20. According to Billings, writing in 1843, the top gable to the south end of the Nine Altars had been completely decayed when it came to be restored in 1827 by Bonomi, and "the present decoration is in imitation of a beautiful Chapel in Gateshead" (i.e. St. Edmund's Chapel). - R.W. Billings, *op.cit.*, 15.
21. *Record* XXXIV.
22. *Record* XXXIV.
23. *Record* XXXIV. The 16th century Screen round the Feretory was given to the University, and in the 1930's sufficient of it survived for it to be copied and the screen renewed in oak round the Feretory.
24. *Record* XXXIV. But Chapter Minutes for 20 July 1845 make it clear that on re-opening the Great West Portal, a "substantial door be placed upon it", i.e. the doorway was not intended to be left open.
25. *Record* XXXIV. The Clock Case was shown in Carter's Long Section, and Billings' perspective, and was reassembled and restored to its original position in 1936, Stephen Dykes Bower advising.
26. *ACM* 17 Nov. 1849. This reredos panel is now stored in the Quire triforium.
27. *Record* XXXVI. (J.C. Bishop, founder of the firm of organ builders of that name).
28. Record XXXVIII & ACM 17 Dec. 1847. These west windows of the aisles were glazed by Willement of London, and Wailes of Newcastle, but no longer survive in the Cathedral, though descriptions of the windows are given in *History and Directory of Durham*, Francis Whellan & Co. (1894).
29. *ACM* 2 Nov. 1858.
30. *ACM* 6 March 1860. i.e. the Chapter did not accept Scott's proposals, but wished to leave the tower as it had been.
31. The Pelican Lectern was made for Scott in 1876 by Francis Alfred Skidmore of Birmingham. The design was intended to follow the description of the lectern in the *Rites of Durham*.
32. Ewan Christian's report is addressed to the Secretary of the Ecclesiastical Commission. The report is now in private ownership in Midlothian, the present author having been provided with a copy.
33. *Proceedings of Soc. Antiquaries London*. Second Series Vol. XXVIII 1915-16, 44 to 56. One of the three Fellows appointed by the Society of Antiquaries to report on the works at Durham was John Bilson, the foremost archaeological researcher of his time on the Cathedral.

Chapter 4

1. *Rites of Durham* (Surtees Society, 107), ed. J.T. Fowler, 1903.
2. They are briefly described by M. Johnson, 'Recent work on the refectory of Durham Cathedral', *Transactions of the Architectural and Archaeological Society of Durham and Northumberland*, new ser., 1(1968), 86-7. A fine example of a refectory scheme showing both patrons and patron saint is provided by the 13th-century and later paintings at Horsham St Faith Priory (Norfolk); see D. Purcell, 'The priory of Horsham St Faith and its wall paintings', *Norfolk Archaeology*, 35 (1974), 469-73. These

also include an enormous Crucifixion - likewise a standard subject for refectories - and the Rites records a similar painting (of late medieval date?) on the west wall at Durham, 'which pictures have been washed over with Lime, and yet do appear through the Lime.'

3. E. Fernie (1980), *op.cit.*, 49-58.

4. D. Park and P. Welford, 'The medieval polychromy of Winchester Cathedral', in *Winchester Cathedral: Nine Hundred Years*, ed. J. Crook (forthcoming),

5. See J. Haselock and D. O'Connor, 'The medieval stained glass of Durham Cathedral', in *Medieval Art and Architecture of Durham Cathedral*, 109.

6. The Finchale decoration has now almost disappeared, but is known e.g. from a watercolour by H.M. Office of Works date 1924 (I am grateful to David Sherlock for drawing this to my attention). At Durham itself, one further example of 13th century polychromy deserves notice: flesh-tints and other colouring surviving on the carved angels at clerestory level in the choir, dating from the end of the century, and first noted during examination prior to cleaning of the vault in 1990.

7. See D. Park, 'Romanesque wall paintings at Ickleton', in *Romanesque and Gothic: Essays for George Zarnecki* (Woodbridge 1987), 159-69; and S. Rickerby and D. Park, 'A romanesque *Visitatio Sepulchri* at Kempley', *Burlington Magazine*, 133 (1991), 27-31.

8. For the candlestick, and other metalwork which must have contributed greatly to the appearance of the cathedral (and of which the sanctuary ring and ironwork of the south-west doorway are major late 12th-century survivals), see J. Geddes, 'The twelfth-century metalwork at Durham Cathedral', in *Medieval Art and Architecture at Durham Cathedral*, 140-8, and *idem*. 'The sanctuary ring of Durham Cathedral', *Archaeologia*, 107 (1982), 125-9.

9. See M. Camille, *The Gothic Idol: Ideology and Image-making in Medieval Art*, Cambridge 1989, 230-2.

10. See C. Wilson, 'The Neville Screen', in *Medieval Art and Architecture at Durham Cathedral*, 90-104.

11. All the wall paintings in this chapel are discussed in detail by D. Park, 'The wall paintings in the Galilee Chapel of Durham Cathedral', in *Friends of Durham Cathedral, Fifty-seventh Annual Report*, 1990, 21-34.

12. P. Welford, 'An investigation into the phenomenon of dark flesh areas in English medieval wall paintings' (unpubl. diss., Conservation of Wall Painting Department, Courtauld Institute of Art, 1991), 4-9, pls. 14-17.

13. For the many brasses that once gleamed from the floor of the cathedral, but were mostly ripped up after the Reformation, see, e.g., J. Coales, ed., *The Earliest English Brasses: Patronage, Style and Workshops 1270-1350*, London, 1987. See also, A. Martindale, 'Patrons and minders: the intrusion of the secular into sacred spaces in the late Middle Ages', in *The Church and the Arts* (Studies in Church History, 28), ed. D. Wood, Oxford 1992, 143-78, for a useful general discussion of secular imagery in churches at this period.

14. The paintings underwent conservation in 1983 by the Canterbury Cathedral Wallpaintings Workshop, and the above account draws heavily in its dating of the paintings and in other aspects on the Workshop's unpublished report by F. Allardyce, L. Medhurst and T. Organ. The hymn was identified by Martin Snape, and the indigo by Helen Howard ('Blue pigments in English medieval wall painting', unpubl. diss., Conservation of Wall Painting Department, Courtauld Institute of Art, 1988, 42-3, ills. 62-9).

Chapter 5

1. N. Pevsner (revised E. Williamson) *op.cit.*, 174.

2. *Ibid*, 178.

3. Kenneth John Conant, *Carolingian and Romanesque Architecture 800-1200* (The Pelican History of Art, Penguin Books: London, Second integrated paperback edition, 1990), 459.

4. A.W. Clapham, *Romanesque Architecture in Western Europe* (Clarendon :Oxford, 1934), 148.

Chapter 6

1. M. Hardie. *Watercolour Painting in Britain*, Batsford: London, vol II (1967) 228-9.

2. I. Curry discusses the pinnacles in his Durham Cathedral lecture, *Durham Cathedral and its Architects*. (1985), 15.

3. Farington is quoted in A. Wilton. *Turner in his Time*. Thames and Hudson: London (1987) 42.

4. I. Curry, *op.cit.*, 22.

5. *Turner and Architecture*, Catalogue of an exhibition at the Tate Gallery, London. 28 March-10 July 1988 No.14.
6. L. Binyon, *John Crome and John Sell Cotman*, Shelley and Co.: London (1897), 56.
7. T. Sharp, *Cathedral City, A Plan for Durham*, Architectural Press: London (1945), 75.
8. H.L. Mallalieu, *Understanding Watercolours*, Antique Collectors Club: London (1985), 66 and 67.
9. J.B. Priestley, *English Journey*, Heinemann: London (1934), 321.
10. *Drawings by Dennis Creffield: English Cathedrals*: Catalogue of a touring exhibition for the South Bank Centre, London (1987) 8 and 24.
11. *An Emotional Response to Durham Cathedral: Paintings and Drawings by Maureen Enright*, Catalogue of an exhibition held at the Leamington Spa Art Gallery and Museum. 8-29 October 1983.
12. *Durham Cathedral Paintings by Birtley Aris*, Catalogue of an exhibition held in Durham Cathedral. 17 July - 14 August 1990. 5.
13. D. Whetstone, "A Really Great Year", *Arts North*, September 1987, 3.
14. Cathedral Residency Publicity Sheet, 1992. 2.
15. George Pattison. "Elizabeth Frink Talks About Art and the Church". *Modern Painters*, II No. 3, (Autumn 1989), 53-57.

Chapter 7

1. On monastic cathedrals see D. Knowles, *The Monastic Order in England*, (Cambridge, 1950), 619-31.
2. In English secular cathedrals the fabric was normally the responsibility of the chapter, but in London one part of St Pauls, the Old Fabric, was the bishop's responsibility, see Kathleen Edwards, *The English Secular Cathedrals in the Middle Ages*, (Manchester, 1967), 231-2.
3. This is more fully examined in A.J. Piper, "The first generations of Durham monks and the cult of St Cuthbert", in *St Cuthbert, his cult and his community to AD 1200*, ed. G. Bonner, D. Rollason and C. Stancliffe, Boydell Press, Woodbridge (1989), 437-46.
4. For the political background see W.E. Kapelle, *The Norman Conquest of the North: the region and its transformation 1000-1135.* (London, 1979).
5. M.G. Snape, "Documentary evidence for the building of Durham cathedral and its monastic buildings", *Medieval Art and Architecture*, op.cit., 20-36, esp.20.
6. F. Barlow, *William Rufus*, (Berkeley & Los Angeles, 1983), 60-1, 74-7, 81-9, 292-4.
7. T. Arnold ed., *Symeonis Monachi Opera Omnia*, (Rolls Series [75], 1882-5), i, 128-9.
8. *Ibid.*, i, 123.
9. *Ibid.*, 139-40.
10. James Raine (ed.), *Historiae Dunelmensis Scriptores Tres*, (Surtees Soc. 9, 1839), 11.
11. J.T. Fowler (ed.), *Rites of Durham*, (Surtees Soc. 107, 1903), 149-50; the original indulgence is Durham Dean & Chapter Muniments Misc. Ch. 1512.
12. James Raine (ed.), (1839) *op.cit.*, 41.
13. J.T. Fowler (ed.), *op.cit.*, 148-9; the original is Durham Dean & Chapter Muniments Misc. Ch. 1518.
14. James Raine (ed.), (1839) *op.cit.*, 91.
15. *Ibid.*, 46, 131-2, cxlii, 135-6, 153.
16. *Ibid.*, ccxvii-iii, cccxxxiv-v.
17. Barbara Harbottle, "Bishop Hatfield's visitation of Durham Priory in 1354", *Archaeologia Aeliana*, 4th series 36 (1958), 99-100. For the massive contribution that Bishop Wykeham of Winchester required the monks of his cathedral to make towards repairing and restoring its fabric, see Joan Greatrex, "A fourteenth-century injunction book from Winchester". *Bulletin of the Institute of Historical Research*, 50 (1977), 242-6, esp. p. 245.
18. James Raine (ed.), *Wills and Inventories ... of the northern counties* i, (Surtees Soc. 2, 1835), 88 (from Durham Dean & Chapter Muniments Misc. Ch. 2622).
19. W.E. Lunt, *Financial Relations of the Papacy with England to 1327*, Medieval Academy of America publication no. 33, (Cambridge, Mass., 1939), 20-22. *Scriptores Tres*, lii-iii.
20. The original account-rolls and rentals are Durham Dean & Chapter Muniments; for extracts, particularly those relevant to building-work, see J.T. Fowler ed., *Extracts from the Account Rolls of the Abbey of Durham*, ii (Surtees Soc. 100, 1899), 372-419.
21. F.M. Powicke and C.R. Cheney, *Councils and Synods*, II: 1205-1313, (Oxford, 1964), 363-4.
22. J.T. Fowler (ed.), 1899, *op.cit.*, 414, 416, 418, 420-5, 440-83. *Symeon*, 139-40.
23. James Raine (ed.), 1835, *op.cit.*, i, 1-5, 11-13, 21, 23, 25-6, 36-8, 43-4, 88.

24. J.T. Fowler (ed.), 1899, *op.cit.*, 400, 408; James Raine (ed.), 1839, *op.cit.*, cxlviii-cliii.

25. The deeds pertaining to the sacrist's estate were kept separately in the Middle Ages, and a separate cartulary was compiled, now Ushaw College MS 25. The deeds remain a separate class in Durham Dean & Chapter Muniments. See *ibid.*, for wax, 4.1.Sacr.8, 12, 15, 4.3.Sacr.11; for lights, 3.1.Sacr.15, 1.2.Sacr.37, 4.3.Sacr.10; "ad operacionem ecclesie", 3.3Sacr.8; for the fabric, 3.1.Sacr.18, 4.3.Sacr.7; for the new fabric, 4.2.Sacr.2.

26. For a general account of developments in England see R.A.R. Hartridge, *A History of Vicarages in the Middle Ages*, (Cambridge, 1930), For Durham Priory's churches see R.A. Lomas and A.J. Piper (eds.), *Durham Cathedral Priory Rentals I: Bursars Rentals*, (Surtees Soc. 198, 1989), 224-7.

27. Durham Dean & Chapter Muniments, 2.1.Pont.14 , 3.2.Pont.8.

28. Durham Dean & Chapter Muniments, 1.10.Pont.2.

29. R.A. Lomas and A.J. Piper (eds.), *op.cit.*, 222.

30. J.T. Fowler (ed.), 1899 *op.cit.*, ii, 372.

31. For fund-raising tours, see F. Barlow, *The English Church 1066-1154*, (London & New York, 1979), 200-1; for a possible 12th-century Durham example, Jas Raine (ed.), *Reginaldi monachi Dunelmensis Libellus de Admirandis Beati Cuthberti Virtutibus ...*, (Surtees Soc. 1, 1835), 109-11. For contributions levied from Durham's cell at Finchale, see Jas Raine ed., *The Priory of Finchale*, (Surtees Soc. 6, 1837), xci, xcvii, both towards the costs of the Neville Screen, and ccxi, for the bell-tower.

32. Except where indicated subsequent statements about monks are drawn from my full typescript biographies.

33. A.J. Piper, *The Durham Monks at Jarrow*, (Jarrow Lecture 1986), 39 n. 55.

34. M.R. Foster, "Durham monks at Oxford c.1286-1381: a house of studies and its inmates", *Oxoniensia* 55 (1990), 99-114; R.B. Dobson, *Durham Priory 1400-1450*, (Cambridge, 1973), 343-59.

35. James Raine (ed.), (1839), *op.cit.*, 130-55.

36. James Raine (ed.), *Dialogi Laurentii Dunelmensis monachi ac prioris*, (Surtees Soc. 70, 1880), 8-13, 27-30.

37. J.T. Fowler (ed.), *op.cit.*, eg. 30.

38. For a striking late fifteenth-century example of an obsessive concern for the size of ecclesiastical buildings and little else about them, see J.H. Harvey (ed.), *William Worcestre: Itineraries*, (Oxford, 1969), e.g. 224-9.

39. For a fuller discussion, see Dobson, 11-32.

40. J.T. Fowler (ed.), op.cit., 102-3; C.F. Battiscombe ed., *The Relics of St Cuthbert*, (Durham, 1956), 79-83.

41. D. Marcombe, *The Dean and Chapter of Durham 1558-1603*, (Durham Ph.D. thesis, 1963), 169-77, 202-9.

42. Spectacularly destructive schemes for the improvement of the building, such the removal of the Neville Screen and the Galilee, were never put into effect; the major changes that took place were largely inspired by a spirit of restoration, notably the Laudian reaction that John Cosin embodied in the mid-17th century, and the work under Deans Waddington (1840-69) and Lake (1869-94), which was partly influenced by the Tractarians. See C.J. Stranks, *This Sumptious Church*, (London, 1973), 80, 49-52, 59-62, 90-2, 95-7.

Chapter 8

1. N.R. Ker (ed.) *Medieval Libraries in Great Britain: A List of Surviving Books*, Royal History Society: London, (2nd edn., 1964), 60-74; see also A.J. Piper's 1987 supplement.

2. S.L. Greenslade, "The contents of the library of Durham Cathedral Priory," *Transactions of the Architectural & Archaeological Society of Durham and Northumberland*, 11 (1965) 347-69.

3. J.T. Fowler (ed.), (1903), *op.cit.*

4. A.J. Piper, "The libraries of the monks of Durham", in M.B. Parkes and A.G. Watson (eds.), *Medieval Scribes, Manuscripts and Libraries*, Scolar Press: London, (1978) 213-249.

5. R.A.B. Mynors, *Durham Cathedral Manuscripts to the End of the Twelfth Century*, Oxford University Press, Oxford (1939).

6. G. Bain, *The Methods of Construction of Celtic Art*, Glasgow, (1951); I. Bain, *Celtic Knotwork*, Constable: London (1986).

7. J. Backhouse, *The Lindisfarne Gospels*, Phaidon & British Library: Oxford, (1981).

8. T.J. Brown (ed.), *The Stonyhurst Gospel of St. John*, Roxburghe Club: Oxford, (1969).

9. C.D. Verey T.J. Brown, E.Coatsworth (eds.) *The Durham Gospels* ....., Rosenkilde & Bagger: Copenhagen (1980).
10. T.J. Brown (ed.) *The Durham Ritual* ....., Rosenkilde & Bagger: Copenhagen (1969).
11. M. Gullick, "The scribe of the Carilef Bible: a new look at some late 11th century Durham Cathedral manuscripts", in L.L. Brownrigg, *Mediaeval Book Production: Assessing the Evidence*, Anderson-Lovelace: Los Altos Hills (1990), 61-83.
12. M.B. Parkes, *Pause and Effect: An Introduction to the History of Punctuation in the West*, Scolar Press: Aldershot (1992).
13. A.I. Doyle, "Mediaeval blind stamped bindings associated with Durham Cathedral Priory", in *De Libris Compactis Miscellanen*, Bibliotheca Wittockiana: Brussels (1984), 31-42.

Catalogue of Paintings

Black and White:

Fig. 49 Thomas Hearne (1714-1817) *Durham Cathedral*, watercolour, 14 3/8" x 21 1/4", 37.2 x 53.9cm. Signed and dated 1783. Victoria and Albert Museum, London. (Photo: Victoria and Albert Museum).

Fig. 50 Edward Edwards (1738-1806) *Durham Cathedral*, watercolour, 11 1/2" x 18 4/5", 29.1 x 47.7cm. Signed and dated 1788. Victoria and Albert Museum, London. (Photo: Victoria and Albert Museum).

Fig. 51 Thomas Girtin (1775-1802) *Durham Cathedral and Bridge*, watercolour, 16 3/8" x 21 1/8", 41.6 x 53.7cm. Signed and dated 1799. Victoria and Albert Museum, London. (Photo: Victoria and Albert Museum).

Fig. 52 J.M.W. Turner (1775-1851) *Durham Cathedral from the Bridge*, watercolour, 12" x 16", 30.5 x 41cm. c.1798. Royal Academy of Arts, London. (Photo: Royal Academy of Arts).

Fig. 53 Thomas Girtin (1775-1802) *Durham Castle and Cathedral*, watercolour, 15 1/2" x 21 3/4", 39.4 x 55.2cm. 1799. Victoria and Albert Museum, London. (Photo: Victoria and Albert Museum).

Fig. 54 John Sell Cotman (1782-1842) *Durham Castle and Cathedral*, watercolour, 12 1/2" x 21", 31.9 x 53.4cm. c. 1809-10. Castle Museum, Norwich. (Photo: Norfolk Museums Service).

Fig. 55 J.M.W. Turner (1775-1851) Drawing from the Tweed and Lakes Sketchbook (Finberg Reference XXV) p.12. 14 1/2" x 10 1/2", 36.8 x 26.7cm. 1797. The Turner Collection, Tate Gallery, London. (Photo: Tate Gallery).

Fig. 56 J.M.W. Turner (1775-1851) Drawing from the Tweed and Lakes Sketchbook (Finberg Reference XXV) p.10. 14 1/2" x 10 1/2", 36.8 x 26.7cm. 1797. The Turner Collection, Tate Gallery, London. (Photo: Tate Gallery).

Fig.57 J.M.W. Turner (1775-1851) *Durham Cathedral*, watercolour, 11 1/2" x 17 1/2", 29.5 x 44.2 cm. c.1835. National Gallery of Scotland, Department of Prints and Drawings. (Photo: National Gallery of Scotland).

Fig.58 William Daniell (1769-1837) *Durham*, watercolour, 15 3/4" x 25 7/8", 40 x 65.7 cm. 1805. Victoria and Albert Museum, London. (Photo: Victoria and Albert Museum).

Fig.59 John Pearson (1777-?1813) *Durham Cathedral from the River*, watercolour, 10 1/2" x 12 7/8", 26.7 x 32.7 cm. Victoria and Albert Museum, London. (Photo: Victoria and Albert Museum).

Fig.60 George Fennel Robson (1788-1833) *Durham Cathedral and Castle*, watercolour, 7 9/10" x 14 1/2", 20.1 x 36.1 cm. Victoria and Albert Museum, London. (Photo: Victoria and Albert Museum). Undated.

Fig.61 George Fennel Robson (1788-1833) *Durham Cathedral from Prebends' Bridge*, watercolour, 19" x 30 1/4". The Bowes Museum, Barnard Catle, Co. Durham. (Photo: The Bowes Museum). Undated.

Fig.62 J.W. Carmichael (1800-1868) *Durham*, oil on canvas, 23 7/8" x 36", 60.6 x 91 cm. Signed and dated "J.W. Carmichael (?)1841". Laing Art Gallery, Newcastle upon Tyne, (Tyne and Wear Museums). (Photo: Courtauld Institute of Art).

Fig.63 R.W. Billings (1813-1874) *Durham Cathedral, West View*. Inscribed "Drawn by R.W. Billings, Engraved by George Winter, Durham. Published by Geo. Andrews and R.W. Billings, April 1846". 8" x 6 2/5", 20.5 x 16.3 cm. (Photo: Mick Garland).

Fig.64 Thomas Greenhalgh (1848-1906) *Above the Rooftops*, watercolour, 26" x 38", 66 x 97 cm. Private Collection. (Photo: D. Hudspeth).

Fig.65 Dennis Creffield (b.1931) *The Galilee, Evening*, charcoal, 23" x 33", 58.4 x 84 cm. 1987 Private Collection. (Photo: the artist).

Fig.66 Dennis Creffield (b.1931) *The Central Tower, Durham Cathedral*, 23" x 33", 58.4 x 34 cm. 1987. Artist's Collection. (Photo: the artist).

Fig.67 Virginia Bodman (b.1954) *A Beam*, charcoal, 28" x 39", 71 x 99 cm. 1983. Artist's Collection. (Photo: the artist).

Fig.68 Birtley Aris (b.1927) *The Screen from the Triforium in the North Transept*, watercolour, 30" x 22 2/5", 76 x 57 cm. 1987. Private Collection. (Photo: the artist).

Fig.69 Birtley Aris (b.1927) *The Screen and Choir from the North Transept* Clerestory, watercolour, 30" x 22 2/5", 76 x 57 cm. 1988. Private Collection. (Photo: the artist).

Fig.70 Colin Wilbourn (b.1956) *Kathedra*, sandstone sculpture, 10' x 6' x 4', 305 x 183 x 122 cm. Photographed against the Cathedral, before being moved to its present site on the river bank beyond Prebends' Bridge. Collection of Durham Cathedral. (Photo: the artist).

Colour:

Pl.VI J.M.W. Turner (1775-1851) *Durham Cathedral looking east along the South Aisle*, watercolour, 29 7/8" x 22 7/8", 75.8 x 58.0 cm. 1797-8. The Turner Collection, Tate Gallery, London. (Photo: Tate Gallery).

Pl.VII J.S. Cotman (1782-1842) *Durham Cathedral*, watercolour, 17 1/10" x 13", 43.6 x 33 cm. 1806. British Museum, London. (Photo: British Museum).

Pl.VIII Felix Mendelssohn Bartholdy (1809-1847) *Durham*, watercolour, 23 x 19cm., 1829. Bildarchiv Preussischer Kulturbesitz, Berlin. (Photo: Bildarchiv Preussischer Kulturbesitz).

Pl.IX Maureen Enright (b.1943) *Cathedral*, oil on canvas, 54" x 36", 137.1 x 91 cm. 1982. Artist's Collection. (Photo: the artist).

Pl.X Robert Soden (b.1955) *God's Factory at Night*, gouache, 39 2/5" x 27 3/5", 100 x 70 cm. 1982. St. Chad's College, Durham. (Photo: the artist).

Select Bibliography

C. Alington, *Durham Cathedral: the Story of a 1000 Years*, Savile Press: Eton (1948).

Patricia R. Andrew (ed) *Durham Cathedral: Artists and Images*, Durham County Council (1993).

R.W. Billings, *Architectural Illustrations and Description of the Cathedral Church at Durham*, London (1843).

I. Curry, "Aspects of the Anglo-Norman design or Durham Cathedral", *Archaeologia Aeliana*, 5th Series, LIV (1986), 31-48.

Durham Cathedral, Topographical Prints from 16th to 20th Centuries, Exhibition Catalogue, Sunderland Art Gallery (February 1969).

J.T. Fowler (ed.), *Rites of Durham*, Surtees Society, vol.107 (1903).

W. Greenwell, *Durham Cathedral* (6th edition, 1904).

G.M. Hills, "The cathedral and monastery of St Cuthbert at Durham", *Journal of the British Archaeological Association*, XXII (1866) 197-237.

C.C. Hodges, "Durham Cathedral", *The Builder*, LXIV, No.2626, (1893), 427-32.

W. Hutchinson, *History of Durham* (1787) Vol 2, 61-270.

M.J. Jackson (ed), *Engineering a Cathedral*, Thomas Telford, Ltd., London (1993).

Medieval Art and Architecture, in *British Archaeological Conference Transactions for 1977* (1980).

W. Page (ed.), *Victoria County History of the Counties of England: Durham*, (London, 1928), vol. III, 96-136.

N. Pevsner (revised by E. Williamson), *The Buildings of England: County Durham* Penguin: Harmondsworth (1983), 162-209.

D. Shipley, *Durham Cathedral*, Tauris Parke: London (1990).

C.J. Stranks, *This Sumptuous Church*, S.P.C.K.: London (1973).

Notes on Contributors

Rosalind Billingham, B.A., M.Phil. taught Art History at Sunderland College of Art and, for many years, at Coventry Polytechnic. She has curated two exhibitions on English painting, co-edited a book on Coventry's architecture, and published articles on art criticism and art education.

Sherban Cantacuzino, C.B.E., M.A., FRIBA began his professional career as a practising architect and writer on architecture. He was executive editor of the *Architectural Review* from 1973-79; his most recent book is *Re-Architecture: Old Buildings, New Uses* (Thames & Hudson, 1989). He has been Secretary of the Royal Fine Art Commission since 1979 and Chairman of ICOMOS UK from 1987. He is also on the executive committee of ICOMOS International in Paris. He is a patron of the City of Durham Trust.

Ian Curry, Dip. Arch., FRIBA, FSA has been in practice as an architect since 1956, based in Newcastle-upon-Tyne and specialising in work on historic buildings and churches. He was appointed Consultant Architect for Durham Cathedral in 1976, and has held similar posts for Carlisle Cathedral since 1982 and Selby Abbey from 1985. He was president of the Ecclesiastical Architects and Surveyors Association, 1969-70 and 1988-89. He has been a member of the Cathedrals Commissions for England from 1981 and a member of the Advisory Board for Redundant Churches since 1990.

Roger Norris, M.A., Dip.Lib. came to Durham in 1966 where he is Deputy Librarian to the Dean and Chapter of Durham, a Vice-President of the Architectural and Archaeological Society of Durham and Northumberland, a member of the Durham Diocesan Advisory Committee for the Care of Churches and a Trustee of the City of Durham Trust.

David Park, M.A., FSA is Director of the Conservation of Wall Painting Department, Courtauld Institute of Art (University of London). He has published widely on English medieval wall paintings, and is coordinator of the National Survey of Medieval Wall Painting (a joint project of the Courtauld Institute and the Royal Commission on the Historical Monuments of England).

Alan J. Piper, M.A. was appointed to Durham University's Department of Palaeography and Diplomatic in 1968. Since then he has worked principally on the medieval archives of the cathedral, and in particular on the very extensive financial records surviving from the later Middle Ages.

Douglas Pocock, M.A., Ph.D. is Reader in Geography and Vice-Principal of St. Chad's College in the University of Durham. He taught at the universities of St. Andrew's and Toronto before moving to Durham in 1972. He is author of two textbooks and over a hundred articles in geographical and planning journals, besides several books on Durham city and county. He has been secretary of the local civic amenity society, the City of Durham Trust, since 1973.

Malcolm Thurlby, Ph.D., FSA, was educated at the University of East Anglia and is now Associate Professor of Visual Arts at York University, Ontario. He has written many articles on English medieval architecture and sculpture, and on 19th-century Canadian architecture.